IMAGES
of America

ALEXANDRIA
POLICE DEPARTMENT

In December 1911, Alexandria police officers were joined by police commissioners in front of the police station at 126 North Fairfax Street. Police headquarters operated there from the department's founding in 1870 until 1959. The old station house is now part of Alexandria City Hall. From left to right are (seated) Commissioners Robert E. Knight, Ned Shinn, and George Schwarzmann, and police captain Charles T. Goods; (standing) Lt. Frank Bettis, policemen John Kerns, James Roland, James Talbert, Banner Young, Charles Bell, Julian Rawlett, Robert H. Cox, Nathan Nicholson, John Roberts, and Walker Campbell, Lt. William Wilkinson, Will Ferguson, Fred Garvey, Sam Reed, Sgt. Wilmer Scott, and policemen Rudolph Norris, Christopher Gill, and Charles G. Miller.

ON THE COVER: Taken in October 1927, this official police photograph features the entire Alexandria Police Department and its fleet in front of police headquarters. The engraved block above the doorway identifying the building as the police station is still visible today, though police use of the building ended in 1959.

IMAGES
of America

ALEXANDRIA
POLICE DEPARTMENT

The Alexandria Police Association

ARCADIA
PUBLISHING

Published by Arcadia Publishing
Charleston, South Carolina

Library of Congress Catalog Card Number: 2006928117

For all general information contact Arcadia Publishing at:
Telephone 843-853-2070
Fax 843-853-0044
E-mail sales@arcadiapublishing.com
For customer service and orders:
Toll-Free 1-888-313-2665

Visit us on the Internet at www.arcadiapublishing.com

*To all faithful members of the Alexandria Police Department,
past, present, and future.*

CONTENTS

Acknowledgments   6

Introduction   7

1.   Uniforms, Badges, and Equipment   9

2.   Cruisers and Stations   23

3.   Investigations   39

4.   Special Operations and Events   53

5.   Traffic Safety   67

6.   Support and Community Services   83

7.   Chiefs, Fallen Heroes, and Trailblazers   97

8.   Off-Duty   115

ACKNOWLEDGMENTS

The Alexandria Police Association gratefully acknowledges those people who graciously shared their photographs, memories, or family history with us. They are Carol Adcock-Stearns, Randy Benarick, Ken Benson, Judy Birney, Ralph Carlton, John Cox, George W. Crump, Jenny Cutright, Dayle Dooley, Curt Eaby, Ron Graves, Norman Grimm, Hope R. Harrington, Bob Harris, Rod Harris, Sandra Holt, Ken Howard, Harry and Charlene Lane, Danny Page, Kathy Salvas, Joe Seiffert, and Lois Smith.

We also appreciate the assistance of the Alexandria Library Special Collections staff, the Alexandria Black History Museum staff, the Alexandria Police Youth Camp board members, and the Alexandria Retired Police, Fire, and Sheriff Association membership. We would like to thank police staff including Chief Charles E. Samarra, Deputy Chief David P. Baker, Deputy Chief Earl Cook, Deputy Chief Blaine Corle, Capt. John Crawford, Lt. Brett Hoover, Lt. Louie Pellegrino, Sgt. Dave Shepherd, Investigator Garry Ground, Officer Gregg Ladislaw, Officer Renzo Torchiani, Special Police Officer Tony Gabriel, Ashley Hildebrandt, Romie Holmes, and Amy Bertsch for their contributions.

INTRODUCTION

The history of law enforcement in Alexandria, Virginia, is as rich as that of the city itself. Located on the Potomac River, just outside of Washington, D.C., Alexandria is considered the hometown of George Washington and Robert E. Lee. It has evolved from an 18th-century seaport town to a struggling community that was home to both the railroad and waterfront industries to a thriving city that values its historic resources, high-tech companies, and diverse population.

Alexandria, twice named an All-America City, has fallen under different flags in its 250-plus-year history, first under England before the American Revolution, then from 1801 to 1847 under Washington, D.C., and finally under Virginia. As early as 1780, Alexandria employed daytime policemen and two night watchmen. By 1797, it had organized a full night watch with watchmen, paid $150 annually, who, according to a town council action, were "to patrol and take charge of such disorderly and suspicious persons." Constables and later policemen were responsible for law enforcement during daylight hours, and this system continued until the Civil War.

Alexandria rejoined the commonwealth in 1847, and when Virginia seceded in 1861, Alexandria, as part of the Confederacy, was quickly occupied by Union forces, who remained there throughout the war. Following Reconstruction, Virginia rejoined the Union, and Alexandria's police force was reorganized. On July 15, 1870, city leaders ended the night watch system, dismantled the daylight police force, and formally authorized the creation of the Alexandria Police Department. By the end of the month, a captain, lieutenant, and 19 policemen were on duty.

Police in the riverfront town faced challenges ranging from petty thieves to drunken sailors to the occasional murder. The police station, jail, and court were housed on North Fairfax Street in the present-day city hall. At the station house, the senior officer kept an activity log and recorded arrests, weather conditions, and criminal offenses. Death sentences were carried out nearby, with hangings in 1873 and 1908. In 1897, a lynch mob overtook the station, removed a prisoner, and killed him at the corner of King and Fairfax Streets.

By the early 1900s, Alexandria, a few dozen streets blocked in a grid, looked toward expansion. In 1915 and 1930, the city annexed the railroad communities of St. Elmo, Rosemont, and Potomac from Arlington and soon doubled in size. Police needed motorized vehicles to reach the residential area today known as Del Ray, and the department hired more officers to serve the outlying area. Police were tasked with enforcing Prohibition laws, and as road accidents resulted in more injuries and deaths, traffic safety became a priority.

In the 1930s, the department took major steps to improve and professionalize itself and its services. It implemented a system to photograph suspects and record their physical attributes. The commanders also opened a week-long training program that all recruits would be required to pass before joining the force. In the late 1930s and early 1940s, radios installed in scout cars improved communication between headquarters and officers, though most policemen remained on foot patrol and relied on call boxes. By the mid-1940s, the department established quick communication with District police and other agencies through a radio system and a Teletype machine.

In 1952, Alexandria expanded again, annexing an eight-square-mile tract to the west from Fairfax County. Though sparsely populated, the West End required a significant increase in police power and resources. The number of patrol cars soon surpassed the motorcycle fleet, and the department quickly outgrew the old station house on North Fairfax. In May 1959, the department moved to 400 North Pitt Street, its new headquarters with holding cells, a radio room, roll-call space, a parking lot, and its own gas pumps.

New tactics emerged, and a canine unit was established in 1959 and yielded immediate results with the capture of felons and rescues of lost children. Efforts to professionalize police service continued, and though new officers were receiving a week of training in Richmond, the need for stronger education was clear. In 1965, Alexandria joined the Arlington and Fairfax County police departments in opening the Northern Virginia Police Academy in Fairfax. All new officers began receiving intensive and consistent training in basic criminal law, physical fitness, search and arrest techniques, firearms use, emergency vehicle operation, and traffic safety.

The 1960s in Alexandria saw both the positive change of the civil rights movement and the emergence of drug abuse and increased street crime. When racial issues caused sporadic crowd disturbances, the department established a community relations team dedicated to improving communication between the police and minorities. With a rise in vice-related crimes in Alexandria's downtown district, police worked to shut down gambling operations, unlicensed wine houses, and illegal massage parlors. Soon gun violence was taking its toll, and the annual homicide rate routinely reached double digits.

In the 1970s, the department organized a group of officers with special tactical training. Equipped with high-powered weapons and protective helmets, the Special Operations Team was deployed to critical incidents like hostage situations. Improvements came to communications with the implementation of the 911 emergency number and computer-aided dispatching in the 1980s.

Alexandria's population grew significantly, especially in the West End, where high-rise apartments soon became home to thousands. The force had grown from 80 officers in 1952 to 180 by 1970 and to 347 sworn and civilian employees by 1983. Plans to build a new, modern police headquarters began in the early 1980s, and the location on Mill Road, outside of Old Town, ensured adequate parking for the growing fleet of cruisers. In 1987, the police department moved into its third headquarters in a complex that houses the city detention center and the sheriff's office.

In the 1980s and 1990s, technology greatly enhanced police service through 911, computer-aided dispatch, and improved crime databases. When the devastation and violence of the crack cocaine epidemic hit Alexandria, police used undercover detectives and remote surveillance to target dealers. The need for police in the community yielded a new approach in which officers were assigned full-time to at-risk neighborhoods and, in some cases, police officers moved into public housing, living as both neighbors and protectors.

Through innovative tactics, high-visibility patrols, crime prevention efforts, and community outreach, serious crime fell steadily. Today Alexandrians enjoy a high quality of life, thanks largely to the work of their police officers. With more than 450 officers and civilian employees, the Alexandria Police Department is again planning to move to a new headquarters, expected to be built in the center of the city within the next 10 years.

The Alexandria Police Association, established in 1927, takes tremendous pride in the dedication of its members and their service to the people of Alexandria. It is much honored to share the history of the Alexandria Police Department through photographs, artifacts, and the experiences of its members.

One

Uniforms, Badges, and Equipment

When an act by the city's board of aldermen and common council officially authorized the Alexandria Police Department in 1870, it also clearly specified the badge symbolizing the officers' authority. The act stated that each "policeman and officer shall wear a badge in the form of a star, made of block tin, not less than two and a half inches in diameter, and numbered in the centre, which said badges shall be furnished at the cost of the city, and be delivered up by all persons using the same when their official connection with the police force ceases." The first badges included when the department was formally organized—July 15, 1870—and featured the state seal and motto "Sic Semper Tyrannis" in the center. Officers wore this badge design until around 1900. A commemorative badge with the original design was issued in 1995 to celebrate the department's 125th anniversary. The one seen here is an authentic 19th-century badge.

The earliest known photograph of the Alexandria Police Department was taken on February 22, 1888, in front of police headquarters, then housed in the 100 block of North Fairfax Street. Officers assembled on this day for the annual parade in honor of George Washington's birthday. Festive bunting adorned the police station as part of the celebration. Officers were required to pay for their own uniforms and firearms. In the doorway is policeman John Nightingale. In the

foreground are, from left to right, policemen Patrick Hayes, William Bontz, Stephen Taylor, Gilbert Simpson, James McCuen, William Price, Samuel Ticer, and William "Cudge" McGrady, Chief James F. Webster, Mayor Emanuel E. Downham, Lt. James Smith, and policemen B. Franklin Bettis, Keith Davis, Rolla "Rolley" Henry, George Jones, Banner Young, Joshua Sherwood, and Cassius "Cash" Brenner.

By the beginning of the 20th century, police uniforms began to change. In both of these images taken around 1905, officers were wearing smaller badges, uniforms styled as suits, and taller hats called helmets. A commanding officer had to inspect each policeman before he went on duty, checking his personal appearance and the condition of his badge, baton, and whistle. Officers were permitted to use their batons only in cases of self-defense or when facing violent or forcible resistance. At least one man who failed to cooperate was rendered unconscious after being struck with a baton and had to be transported to the police station in a wheelbarrow. (Top image: Alexandria Library Special Collections.)

Officers began wearing a different badge around 1900. This one is from the department's historical collection. The new design was significantly smaller and no longer featured a star nor the date of the department's founding. The state seal and motto were far more detailed but would be replaced in future designs by the seal of Alexandria.

The department's collection includes these antique handcuffs, both commonly used throughout the country. Produced by Bean's and patented in 1899, the pair on top cost about $4. The lower pair, produced by the Peerless Handcuff Company, date to around 1914. The patented design was the first with a swing-through bow. This revolving mechanism allowed an officer to easily close the cuffs around a prisoner's wrist.

Officers had to pay for their own uniforms. To help raise money, they hosted annual benefit excursions, selling tickets to local merchants. In the summer of 1915, about the time this photograph was taken, their excursion was an outing to Marshall Hall, a popular picnic area and entertainment pavilion across the Potomac in Maryland. With their uniform jackets open, the policemen appear to be relaxing along the waterfront.

In 1909, city leaders approved funding to furnish each officer with a new revolver. Before that, officers had to provide their own sidearms and ammunition. In 1911, military-style caps replaced the old helmets, and by the time this photograph was taken around 1920, the dress and weapons had truly become uniform. When one officer was unavailable for this official portrait, the photographer added him later but failed to properly adjust the scale.

Policemen who patrolled on motorcycles were called mounted officers and, later, motormen. They wore uniforms modified for their duty on the road. Seen in these images from around 1923, Lawrence Padgett, one of the earliest motormen, wore pants with a wider seat and thighs and leather gloves and leg wear that added protection from weather and road hazards. The cross-draw holster was popular at the time, especially among motormen. A patch representing the motorcycle unit is visible on Padgett's left arm and was the earliest known shoulder patch worn in Alexandria. Padgett served for more than 35 years, rising to the rank of lieutenant.

In 1927, the uniforms were modified again. In the fall of that year, all officers assembled in front of headquarters wearing "metropolitan blue" and displaying their fleet of four motorcycles and a patrol wagon. From left to right are (seated) are policeman Charles Stewart, Lt. William Wilkinson, Capt. William Campbell, councilmen George Jones and Thomas Fannon, Mayor William Smoot, city manager Paul Morton, councilmen J. E. W. Timberman and Edward Ticer,

policeman Charles McClary, and Sgts. Edgar Sims and Heber Thompson; (standing) Andrew Travers and policemen Claude Meade, Wesley Snoots, Ernest Wright, Charles Summa, Charles Miller, Elton Hummer, Richard Payne, Harry Glossom, Lawrence Padgett, Ernest Suthard, Clarence McClary, George Everly, Richard Eberhardt, George Drumheller, Julian Rawlett, Henry Taylor, and Ronald Mullen.

Uniformed officers assembled at the corner of North Fairfax and Cameron Streets in this photograph from the early 1950s. Under the blue uniforms, patrolmen wore grey shirts, commanding officers wore white shirts, and all wore ties. Their gun belts, many holding extra ammunition, were secured by an adjustable strap across the chest. Within a few years, the greatest permanent change to the uniform would be the addition of the department shoulder patch. The patch, visible on the arms of two officers in the below image from 1958, is identical to the one worn today. In the back row, wearing a helmet, is Pvt. J. Allen Glass, a member of the motorcycle unit. Motor officers first wore helmets in Alexandria in 1956, though use of full-face versions would be more than two decades away.

While officers have carried handguns since the agency's founding, the department has continually explored the use of other weapons. In the 1920s, police commanders obtained a baton that emitted tear gas upon the push of a button, though there is no indication this device was widely used. Police considered other weapons for controlling unruly crowds where deadly force would not have been justified. In the late 1940s, Det. William Gosney (above) detonated a smoke grenade in a remote location. Officers using gas needed to protect themselves as well, and in 1969, Pvt. Joseph Seiffert (left) and Cpl. Joseph Robey (right) wore masks during a weapons exercise at Jones Point Park. The department also obtained a pepper fogger, which could dispense large amounts of irritating gas at times of civil unrest.

The final badge design was formalized in the early 1920s and has changed very little since then. The badge prominently features the city seal of Alexandria: a ship and balance scales. Officers wear the smaller, silver-colored version, and detectives and ranking officers wear a brass-colored shield with an eagle design. The details of the badge and hat shield are shown in a photograph of Pvt. Claude S. McDonald in the early 1960s. The number two on his badge reflected his seniority at the department. McDonald served for 38 years and directed traffic at King and Washington Streets for many of those years. The J. C. Penney store, then located on North Washington Street, is visible in the background.

Until the late 1960s, officers were required to wear hats and long-sleeved uniform shirts, even in the summer, when temperatures reached the 90s. In the 1950s, the chief considered a short-sleeved option but was concerned that some officers' tattoos might be visible. The uniform was finally modified for warm weather with an open-collar short-sleeved shirt option. In 1978, members of the 4th Platoon wore hats and ties in their official portrait on the steps of headquarters on North Pitt Street. Officer Eric Ratliff (below), in a photograph from around 1980, donned short sleeves and had a wooden baton nearby as he patrolled in his cruiser. Though issued to all officers, hats are not required as part of the daily uniform but must be worn at certain official ceremonies.

As the philosophy of community-oriented policing emerged in the 1990s, more Alexandria officers returned to walking their beats, and some patrolled on bicycles. Those on bikes were permitted to wear shorts, like officers Willie McMeans (left) and Shannon Soriano (center), who are assisting citizen Helen Miller (right) at Market Square in this photograph.

Today officers in specialized assignments wear uniforms that enhance their ability to work safely and efficiently. K-9 handlers and members of the Special Operations Team are issued uniforms similar to the battle dress uniforms worn by the military. Ranking officers wear white shirts and blue pants, while line officers wear grey shirts and blue pants. In 1997, when this photograph was taken, a national uniform association named Alexandria the best dressed agency of its size.

Two

CRUISERS AND STATIONS

For nearly 40 years, Alexandria's policemen patrolled the city on foot. In the 1890s, each officer was required to patrol his entire beat four times each shift and was specifically forbidden to linger on his route. Officers on foot, familiar with their beats, took immediate notice of suspicious people or an open door. The introduction of motorized vehicles changed the responsibilities of police officers and the way they did their jobs. Because of the automobile, police were more likely to have contact with citizens involved in accidents or committing traffic violations. Additionally, officers patrolling in their cruisers were less likely to have casual, eye-to-eye contact with the general public. Alexandria police obtained their first motorized vehicle, a motorcycle, in 1918. The following year, they added a motorized patrol wagon. This photograph, from around 1940, shows Lt. Heber Thompson in front of one of the earliest marked Alexandria police vehicles. (Alexandria Library Special Collections.)

When Alexandria's annexation of Potomac became effective in 1930, the size of the city doubled, and officers needed more vehicles to adequately patrol the residential community. This photograph, taken around 1930, reflects the department's entire fleet of a car, six motorcycles, and a patrol wagon. In 1933, the department had three radio-equipped cars, two Fords and one Chevrolet. Each was driven an average of 4,200 miles a month. Another image from the late 1940s was taken of a radio car in front of Union Station. This marked cruiser was also equipped with a siren mounted on the roof.

Throughout the 1930s and 1940s, Alexandria police had more motorcycles than cars. One of the motorcycles ridden by Cpl. Henry Grimm in the late 1930s, possibly a 1934 Harley-Davidson, was equipped with a sidecar. Around 1947, when the below photograph in front of police headquarters was taken, the fleet consisted of two cruisers and eight motorized cycles. From the time of its founding in 1870, the police department was headquartered at 126 North Fairfax Street in a wing of city hall. The station house had an office for the chief, small cells for prisoners, and a desk near the entrance for the duty officer to use. The second floor housed the police court. As the department grew, the station house was renovated and garage space eliminated.

Early firearms training was limited, and for many years, the department used an underground range in a plumber's shop near headquarters. Heading outdoors in 1941, several officers, including, from left to right, Cpl. George Ellmore, Lt. Edgar Sims, Pvt. Thomas McGowan, Pvt. Claude Nixon, Pvt. Robert Jones, Det. Russell Hawes, Pvt. Jack Kelley, Pvt. Thomas Woods, Pvt. William Cator, Pvt. William Schwartz, Pvt. George Jordan, Pvt. Russell Greenwalt, Pvt. Leslie Saunders, Sgt. Joseph Butler, and Sgt. Henry Grimm, take part in experimental training. Detective Hawes, in plain clothes, fires a long gun. At the same training event, Hawes (below, second from left) holds a tommy gun as he inspects his target along the railroad tracks.

As the city grew more densely populated, finding appropriate places for firearms training became more challenging. The department continued to evaluate new weapons, and in the 1950s, Maj. Russell Hawes test fired a gas gun to evaluate it for use in civil disturbances. The department held traditional firearms training at private and military ranges until the late 1950s, when they began using a gravel pit along Shirley Highway. In the 1960s, officers used an outdoor range at Jones Point along the waterfront for pistol and rifle practice, until citizens raised safety and environmental concerns with the National Park Service, which was responsible for the land.

In 1952, Alexandria's annexation of eight square miles from Fairfax County took effect, nearly doubling the size of the city for the second time in 22 years. Though initially sparsely populated, the West End of Alexandria would grow quickly and require additional police resources. The department outgrew its old station house, and in 1959, a new police building opened at 400 North Pitt Street. The red brick structure, seen in this 1959 photograph, cost about $350,000 to build and was three times the size of the old station. It had modern lock-up facilities, interview rooms to question suspects, space for training, a darkroom for film processing, and other special features. Unlike the space on North Fairfax Street, this facility was built for the purpose of housing a police department. The cruisers parked in front were Plymouths, very possibly the Pursuit model, which was specifically developed for police use.

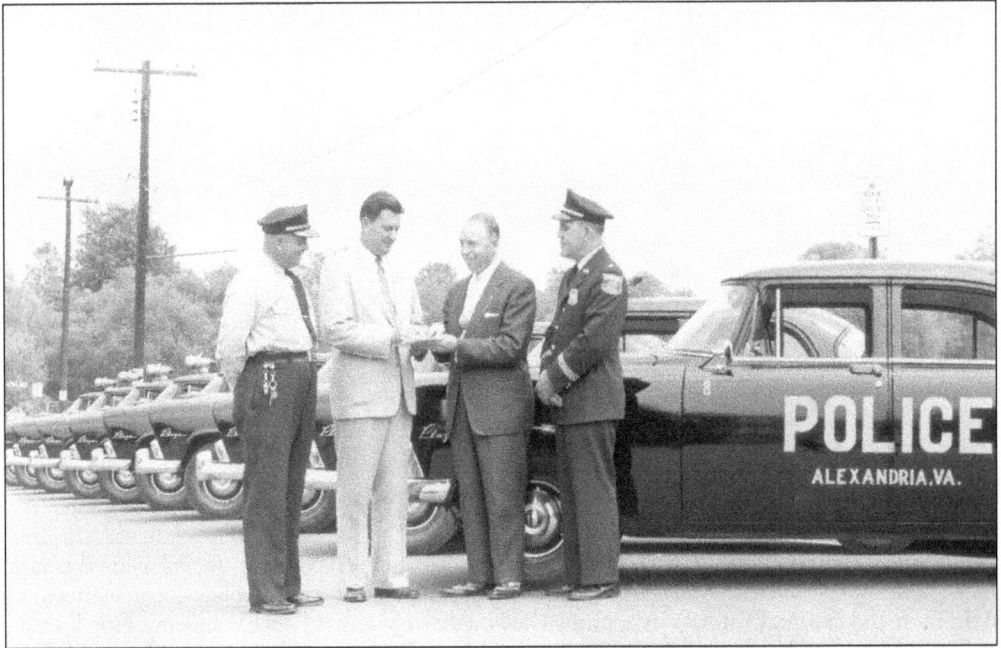

From the late 1950s into the mid-1960s, Alexandria police purchased Plymouth vehicles. Capt. James W. Baber (far left) and Maj. Russell Hawes (far right) were ready to take possession of these new Plymouth Plazas in the late 1950s. Plymouth and other manufacturers began developing special police packages for law enforcement needs and promoted them to the public safety market. The cruisers below on a dark Alexandria street are likely 1958 Plymouth models, which according to performance specifications were capable of traveling from 0 to 60 miles per hour in under eight seconds. A battery-powered spotlight in the roadway served as a flare.

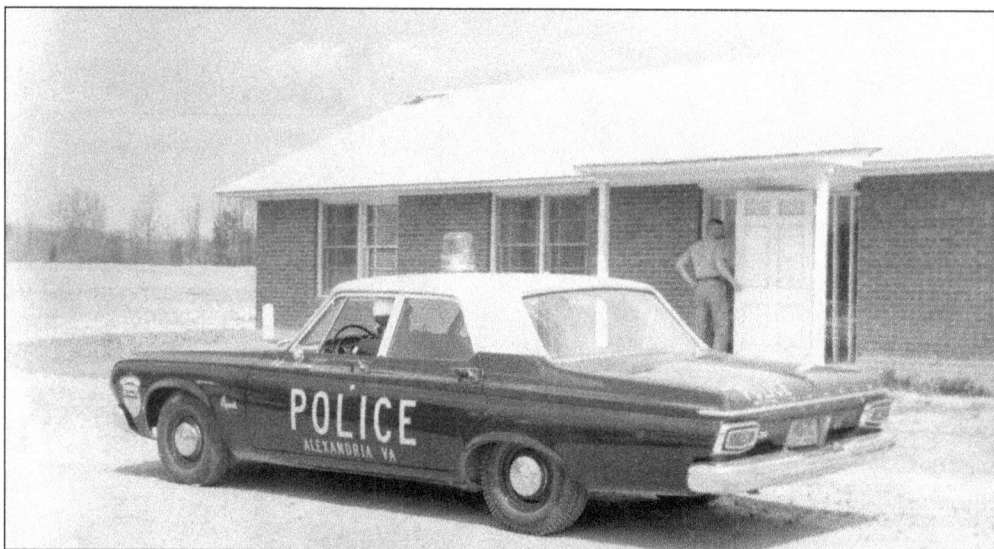

Other than police headquarters and court, the two places where Alexandria officers spend the most time are the police academy and the hospital. In 1965, Alexandria joined police departments from Arlington and Fairfax Counties in opening the Northern Virginia Police Academy. First located on Popes Head Road in Fairfax, it provided more than 350 hours of training to new recruits. This photograph, with Pvt. Edward Bass in the cruiser, shows the academy in its first year. It later moved to Arlington, and today the Northern Virginia Criminal Justice Training Academy is located in Ashburn in Loudoun County. Routine investigations into accidents and assaults bring police to Alexandria Hospital, like this officer in the parking lot. The hospital moved from the 700 block of Duke Street to 4320 Seminary Road in 1962, the year this photograph was taken.

Inside headquarters on North Pitt Street, many officers performed administrative duties, and those at the front desk had significant contact with the public. Citizens coming in the station were greeted by the desk sergeant, and staff fielded calls, dispatched patrol units over the radio, and sent messages to other police departments over a Teletype machine. Officers immediately alerted commanders to serious events or major crimes. A pneumatic tube from the front desk to the records room enabled officers to quickly send paperwork to record clerks. The officers working at the front desk in 1969 are, from left to right, Pvt. George Davis, Pvt. James Richardson, Sgt. Ferdinand Plitt, and Cpl. James Bland, while Sgt. Edgar Cassady looks over documents in the background. About a year after this photograph was taken, Plitt was assigned to a new unit called the community relations team, created to improve department relations with the public, especially with members of the black community.

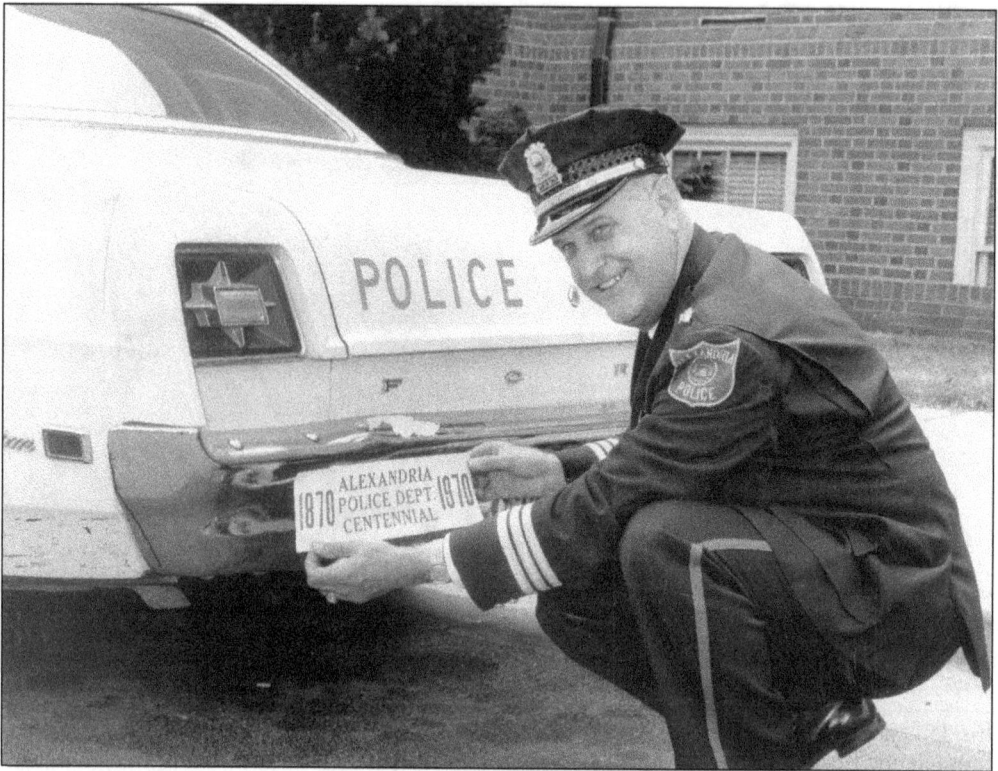

In 1970, the Alexandria Police Department celebrated its 100th anniversary. FBI director J. Edgar Hoover sent the department a letter of congratulations to mark the occasion. Leslie Saunders, who served as acting chief for several months that year, advertised the centennial with a bumper sticker on his Ford cruiser. Saunders joined the department in 1937 and became an inspector before being named interim chief.

Getting into their 1968 Ford Galaxie in front of headquarters are Pvt. Joseph Seiffert (left) and Pvt. Alfred Washington (right). Construction activity is visible in the background of this 1969 image. Within 10 years of moving into the North Pitt Street station, the department needed additional space, and so the second floor was expanded.

The construction at North Pitt Street extended the second floor to the full length of the building. When the renovations were completed, the north wing housed the research and crime prevention unit and the personnel section. The records section was extended into the south wing. Evidence of the construction is apparent on the north wall, where the brickwork differs below the second-floor windows. An aerial photograph from the 1980s looks south over the police department and jail. A line of white cars on North Pitt Street to the left is parked in front of the entrance to headquarters. Other cruisers parked off the street in the back lot behind the jail, which was located on the corner of Princess and North St. Asaph Streets.

For several years after the renovations, patrol officers remained at the North Pitt Street station. This image from around 1970 shows Lt. Russell Greenwalt, a veteran commander, and his workspace. In a squad photograph from 1974, officers assemble in the basement for roll call. The members of the 4th Platoon are, from left to right, (first row) Pvt. Steven Smith, Pvt. Joe Martin, Pvt. John Bell, and Pvt. Donald Charlson; (second row) Pvt. Edward Sarra, Sgt. Harry Lane, Pvt. John Avery, Pvt. Earl Walts, Sgt. Mike Norris, Pvt. Edward Templeman, Pvt. Edward Prokop, and Sgt. Paul Sheehan; (third row) Pvt. Joseph Ennett, Lt. Joseph Seiffert, Pvt. Clyde Bennett, auxiliary Janice Moers, and Pvt. Terry O'Keefe. In the 1980s, when conditions at the North Pitt Street station became too tight, patrol officers moved to a facility near Landmark Mall.

As the department and headquarters grew, so did the police fleet. In early 1960s, Alexandria officers were riding Harley-Davidson Duo-Glides, like this one being ridden by Pvt. Ed Bass near King Street and Russell Road. This model had large boxes on the back for the radio, allowing motor officers the same communication as those in cruisers. Harley-Davidson also made three-wheeled motorized cycles known as Servi-Cars. First produced in the early 1930s, the Servi-Car was added to Alexandria's fleet in the 1940s. Though production of the Servi-Car ceased in the 1970s, Cpl. Ronald Deitz operated his Servi-Car into the early 1980s. One retired Servi-Car from the Alexandria fleet is now in the department's historical collection.

Among the specialized Alexandria police vehicles was this paddy wagon from the early 1970s. Paddy wagons were designed to transport multiple prisoners and are rarely used in Alexandria today. Standing outside city hall on North Royal Street to accept delivery of the paddy wagon are, from left to right, Chief John Holihan, Deputy City Manager Clifford Rusch, Mayor Charles Beatley, Paul Schott (who headed the city's general services), and Capt. James F. Smith.

When the Chrysler Corporation introduced the K-car design around 1980, Alexandria incorporated the new car into its fleet. In this image, the mid-sized sedan faced the 1978 Plymouth Fury, one of the fastest and most popular police cars of the 1970s. In the early 1990s, Alexandria officers drove Chevrolet Caprices until they were discontinued; by the late 1990s, the standard Alexandria patrol cruiser was the Ford Crown Victoria.

After decades of shooting in gravel pits and along the Potomac, Alexandria police opened their own range in 1970. The facility, now shared by Arlington County police, was fairly isolated when it first opened on Eisenhower Avenue, as this image looking northeast shows. The facility is more than 60 yards long and 30 yards wide and has classroom and storage space. Special baffles trap projectiles, preventing bullets from leaving the range, which is enclosed with high masonry walls and secure fencing. The range was renamed in honor of Cpl. Charles W. Hill, a police firearms instructor who was killed in the line of duty in 1989.

The city authorized a new police headquarters to replace the crowded North Pitt Street station and selected a location overlooking the Capital Beltway south of Eisenhower Avenue. The new public safety complex, under construction in this 1986 image, housed the police department, sheriff's office, and jail. Police officially moved into 2003 Mill Road, their third headquarters, in 1987. Despite many modern features, like a state-of-the-art 911 center, the station had greater challenges, like space restraints and a foundation that continued to settle more than 15 years after it was built. As the building undergoes repairs today and plans are underway for a new police facility in the center of the city, many police functions have already moved from Mill Road. Patrol, investigations, and administration operate out of private office space in the Eisenhower Valley. The image below, taken around 2001, shows part of the fleet in front of the Mill Road headquarters.

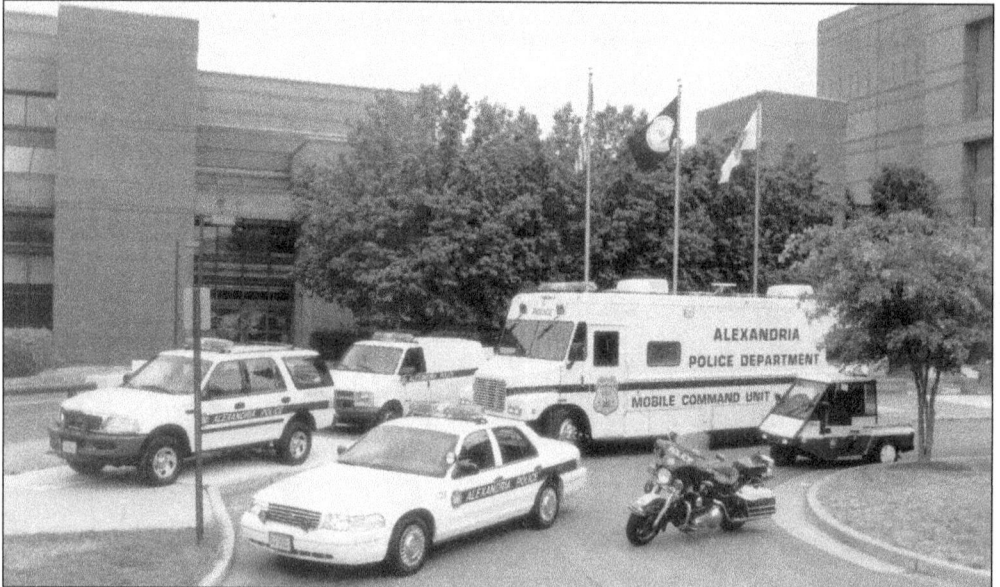

Three

INVESTIGATIONS

Police investigate all types of crimes, from violent offenses to vice activity. Even before the Volstead Act outlawed liquor nationally, Virginia became a dry state in 1916. In Alexandria, police seized illegal whiskey and moonshine and conducted still raids in the city and in Fairfax County. In one week in 1921, Alexandria, Fairfax, and federal authorities seized 11 stills, 2,500 gallons of mash, and 125 gallons of whiskey. Proudly displaying the fruits of their labor are, from left to right, Alexandria police officers Patrick L. Magner and Haywood J. Durrer, federal prohibition agent J. J. Hudgins, and constable Frederick J. Wease of Fairfax. Police had to pay particular attention to activity along the waterfront, as boats smuggled in liquor and housed distilling operations. Durrer became so good at detecting whiskey that he reportedly once found a 25-gallon barrel of whiskey buried four feet underground simply by the odor. Even after Prohibition, Alexandria police conducted raids on illegal wine houses and seized moonshine. One investigation in 1964 ended with raids of 45 homes and businesses and the arrests of 57 people.

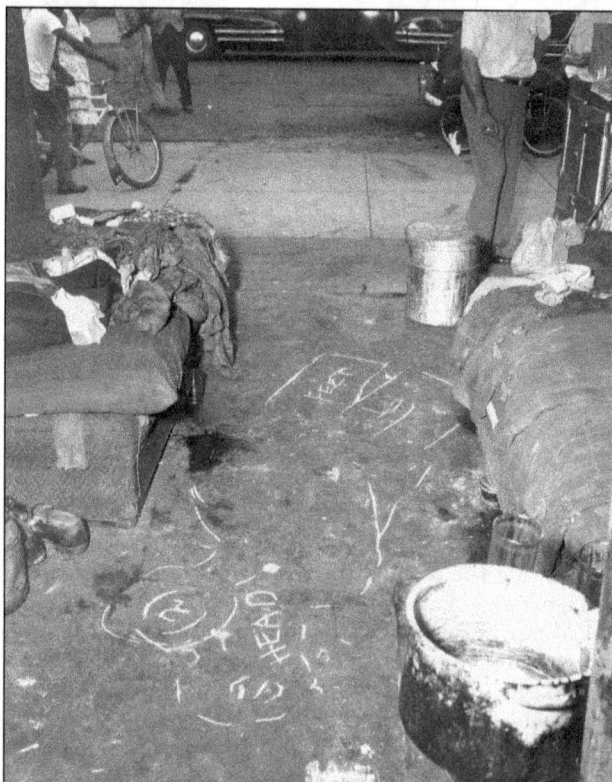

Though burglaries and robberies are far more common than homicides, murder cases attract the most interest from the public and police. Detectives arriving on the scene of a violent death begin their investigation immediately by preserving the crime scene and locating witnesses. These photographs captured the scene of a double shooting in the summer of 1948. The men were inside this garage in the 500 block of North Alfred Street with the garage door open. Another man came to the doorway and began shooting, killing one man and wounding the second. A witness told detectives who the gunman was and that he escaped on a bicycle. He was later arrested. The chalk outlines on the floor mark where each victim was found, and the photographs show the scene from the street and facing the street.

Photography allows police to preserve a crime scene exactly as it was found and clearly identify key locations, such as where people were or where evidence was recovered. In a photograph from 1948, police used circles and initials to mark where two men were when a fight in a Princess Street barber shop turned deadly. In 1952, an Alexandria woman died of complications from an illegal medical procedure. When police interviewed the suspect, they learned where he had discarded the instruments used in the operation. Detectives recovered the evidence along U.S. Route 1. Det. Robert L. Jones, seen in this photograph, points to the specific location, and investigators later marked the exact place by drawing a circle.

Most homicide victims are killed by someone they know, and many murders are motivated by a personal or family relationship. That was the case in 1952, when a man with two female companions inside this parked car was killed. All three had been drinking when one of the women reached into the glove compartment, pulled out a handgun, and shot the man. She ran away but was quickly captured by police. The shooting happened in the afternoon on North West Street and several children on their way home from school stopped by the scene. A 1959 fatal shooting on Rosecrest Avenue was precipitated by an argument about the victim insulting the suspect's father. After the shooting, the suspect cut the telephone line to prevent anyone in the home from calling for help.

Sometimes a single crime can escalate into multiple offenses, and police must document all aspects of the incident. In February 1959, a man reported that someone had broken into his home and assaulted him. Pvt. Bobby G. Padgett responded and located the suspect. As he tried to arrest him, a second officer arrived. A scuffle ensued and the suspect got Padgett's pistol and shot him with it. The second officer and the suspect exchanged gunfire and the suspect ran off. He was captured a few blocks away. When Padgett died, the original burglary became a capital murder case. Police photographs captured key aspects of the incident, including the broken windowpane in the door showing how the suspect got in and the police cruiser where Padgett's gun, the murder weapon, was found.

Violent crime scenes vary as greatly as the cases, from a bar in downtown Alexandria to a family kitchen in a quiet housing development. In 1949, Lt. James W. Baber (left) and Maj. Edgar J. Sims watch as the body of a small child is removed from a home in Cameron Valley. Police arrested the father for fatally shooting all three of his children at breakfast time. Cameron Valley homes were built during World War II to provide housing to military families. In the fall of 1962, police arrested a man for killing a customer inside the Pig Pit, a Queen Street restaurant. The victim was at a table drinking a beer when the suspect shot him dead. Investigators were still reviewing evidence when this photograph was taken.

In every suspicious death investigation, detectives must thoroughly search the scene to find evidence. In the summer of 1973, detectives comb a lot behind East Reed Avenue where a man's body had been found. Detectives used a grid search technique after cordoning off the field strewn with debris. They later arrested a teenager for the fatal stabbing. Today an apartment building and parking garage stand where the litter-filled field was.

In early 1981, Deputy William G. Truesdale was transporting prisoners to the jail when one grabbed Truesdale's gun. The prisoner shot Truesdale in the chest and killed him in an escape attempt. The jail was located very close to the police station, and dozens of officers saturated the area. Police captured the suspect, seen here on the ground, in a parking lot behind the 300 block of North Washington Street.

In the 1950s and early 1960s, police investigated several commercial burglaries in which safes were stolen. In many cases, the thieves were after money stored in the safes, but some targeted drugstore safes to steal narcotics. In the spring of 1961, someone broke into this drugstore in the 4600 block of King Street and stole a safe. Crime photographs documented the store's back exit with an open door and the empty space where the safe had once been. The same store, known as Claremont Rexall, was burglarized again four years later, when someone broke out the window and stole cash and narcotics.

In the fall of 1961, thieves burglarized Gibson's pharmacy in Old Town and stole narcotics. Investigators learned the suspects had hidden the drugs in a wooded area at Jones Point, where the Wilson Bridge was being built. Cpl. Carl Dutzman was on a stakeout when the men returned to dig up the bag of drugs. Dutzman recovered the evidence, and police charged two Alexandrians with illegal possession of narcotics.

When burglars were unable to break into a safe while it was in a business, they would remove it and take it to a different and often remote location. Police recovered safes in cemeteries and woods. This safe was taken from the post office at the Virginia Theological Seminary and discovered in a heavily wooded area along Polk Avenue.

Detectives in the Criminal Investigations Bureau were responsible for investigating major crimes like auto theft, burglary, sexual assault, robbery, and murder. At the start of each shift, detectives attended roll call, which was held in the basement of the North Pitt Street station. Maps on the wall in the background of this image from around 1970 showed where crimes had occurred.

The Youth Bureau handled cases involving juveniles who were runaways, truants, and delinquents. Around 1960, policewomen were hired to investigate juvenile cases, and by 1973, when this photograph was taken, they comprised half of the bureau. From left to right are (first row) Det. Ann Melchior, Det. Charlene Lane, and Sgt. Kathleen Salvas; (second row) Lt. George Thodos, Pvt. Albert Beverly, and Det. Linwood "Marty" West.

One very useful tool detectives use is the polygraph, more commonly known as the lie detector. A trained polygraph examiner asks someone a series of questions, and the polygraph instrument records the examinee's relative blood pressure, respiration, and the amount of moisture on their skin. The examiner then analyzes those responses and determines if the examinee is being truthful or deceptive. Though not often used in court, investigators frequently use the polygraph to help eliminate someone from suspicion or confirm the likelihood of their involvement in a specific crime. Prior to training their first polygraph examiner, Alexandria police transported suspects to Washington, D.C., for a polygraph examination. In this image from 1966, Lt. Roy Canard administers a polygraph examination and analyzes the results as they print out on chart paper. Today polygraph exams are conducted using state-of-the-art computers; however, they still record and analyze the same physiological responses.

Documenting crime scenes and recovering evidence are critical duties in any police investigation. As early as 1927, Alexandria police established a unit specifically for identification purposes. That year, a man arrested for liquor possession gave police a false name but through photographs and fingerprints was positively identified as an escaped convict from North Carolina. By the 1960s, identification technicians, or I.D. techs, were well trained in photography, evidence collection, and latent fingerprint examination. I.D. techs like officer D. Roger Crabtree, shown using a photographic enlarger in this early 1970s image, had cameras, film, and a full darkroom for processing crime-scene photographs. To match latent fingerprints with existing ones on file, officer Harold "Ken" Carpenter (below), in another photograph from the early 1970s, uses a bright lamp and a loupe to closely examine the smallest identifying details.

To properly recover and transport evidence, identification technicians rely on a large vehicle, like this Dodge van parked in front of the police station on North Pitt Street in 1973. The van offered adequate space to store equipment necessary for thorough crime-scene processing. Members of the identification staff are, from left to right, secretary Sue Faunistock, Cpl. Shirley Woodward, Sgt. Ed Streapy, Cpl. Ken Carpenter, and Pvt. Kenneth Howard.

Technicians, like officer Steven Mason in this photograph from around 1980, used a brush and powder to dust for latent fingerprints before lifting the prints for possible identification. For decades, all matches had to be done by hand. In 1984, Alexandria joined five other police departments in establishing the Northern Virginia Regional Identification System, a computer database that searched more than a million fingerprint records in an hour.

The emergence of drugs in the 1960s required a change in police tactics. Officers began working undercover in narcotics investigations and arrested people for distributing marijuana and hashish. Police used some of the drugs they seized in displays to educate the public about the prevalence of narcotics and what different drugs looked like. This display from around 1970 showcased pills, marijuana plants, and even a jar of moonshine.

Narcotics activity resulted in crime, especially in some downtown and greater Del Ray neighborhoods. In the early 1980s, the plainclothes officers in this image were part of the tactical unit used to target street-level crime. It was later disbanded, but a new street crimes unit evolved in 1987, when the crack cocaine epidemic caused an increase in crime.

Four

SPECIAL OPERATIONS AND EVENTS

Whether protecting VIPs or participating in special events, Alexandria police have always been eager to serve, especially in historic events. The unidentified uniformed officer at right assisted with crowd control when royalty visited Northern Virginia. Rambai Barni, the queen of Siam, stands just to the left of the officer on her way to Mount Vernon in the spring of 1931. First Lady Lou Henry Hoover (left of the queen) and their entourage arrived from Washington, D.C., on the presidential yacht, *Sequoia*. They had just left the boat and were walking to George Washington's home when this photograph was taken. Though Mount Vernon is south of Alexandria's city limits, it was not unusual for Alexandria officers to respond to emergencies in Fairfax County in the early 1900s. This officer, a member of the traffic unit, would have been able to travel to Mount Vernon easily on his motorcycle.

With a primary function of traffic enforcement, motor officers have the flexibility to provide escorts or pursue fleeing vehicles. Policeman Wesley Snoots, seen in this 1925 image, was twice struck by cars while on his motorcycle. In 1929, Snoots arrested two men after discovering liquor in their car. He ordered them to drive to the police station as he rode alongside on his motorcycle. When they approached Cameron Street, the suspects turned their vehicle and struck Snoots, knocking him to the ground. Both men fled but were captured in Fredericksburg. In 1932, a reckless driver struck Snoots at North Washington and Queen Streets, causing serious injuries that left him unable to work for a year. Snoots's bravest act was in 1928, as he directed traffic in Rosemont to protect young people sledding on the street. When a car failed to stop at Snoots's direction, he quickly jumped in front of an oncoming sled to keep it from colliding with the car. Left with lacerations and a dislocated shoulder, Snoots was credited with saving the young sledder's life.

As seen in this photograph taken around 1951, motor officers had the safety benefit of windshields, but not helmets. By 1950, the police fleet featured 10 motorcycles, but because accidents left motor officers with serious injuries, the city moved to reduce the number of motor units. Some law enforcement agencies, like the Virginia State Police, phased out the use of motorcycles in the 1950s, and others used them only for parades and special events. But the motorcycles were very useful on crowded streets and allowed officers to maneuver about easily. Alexandria later rebuilt its motor unit. Police motorcycles have remained popular with officers and citizens, especially young ones like those in this 1981 image with officer Edward Sarra on his Harley-Davidson.

Police departments value expert marksmanship among their officers, and in the late 1920s, many large agencies in the country organized competitive pistol teams. By the mid-1930s, Alexandria's force had its own pistol team, which competed against squads from the Virginia State Police, Metropolitan Police, and U.S. Park Police. In the photograph at left, three members of the team, Sgt. George Everly (left), Pvt. George Embrey (center), and Sgt. Edgar Sims, practice their cross-draw and firing techniques. Embrey had previously served as a police officer for the town of Potomac, and after Alexandria officially annexed Potomac in 1930, the city hired Embrey for its force. While with Potomac, Embrey was shot in the face by an assailant, and while with the city police years later, he was knocked off his motorcycle and lapsed into a coma. He recovered from both injuries.

Alexandria's pistol team became highly competitive in the early 1960s, winning many honors. In 1960, Sgt. Marshall Snyder (second from left) presented team members Pvt. Joseph Robey (far left), Pvt. John Cox (second from right), and Pvt. Jim Outland (far right) with yet another trophy. Robey became the range master when the department's shooting range opened in 1970. In 1962, Cox (below), a firearms instructor for the police department, finished first in a competition hosted by the White House. He was also the first police officer in the country to earn top qualifications from the National Rifle Association as a distinguished expert in the law enforcement category.

In 1959, Alexandria became the first department in the metropolitan area to establish a K-9 team. Sgt. Cecil T. Kesler was partnered with King, a jet-black German shepherd. King was a stray at the shelter, and the Animal Welfare League of Alexandria donated him to the police department. Kesler and King trained to search buildings, track criminals, and locate missing people. The team saw immediate success when, in 1960, they cornered a man wanted for robbing a gas station in Fairfax. This photograph was taken moments after the apprehension, and as a Fairfax officer took custody of the prisoner, King kept a close watch while Kesler (far right) held his lead.

In 1960, the Canine Corps grew to six teams. Citizens and local organizations donated the dogs, and each team underwent 14 weeks of training. Officers and dogs studied obedience, tracking, building searches, agility, and apprehension techniques. In a 1962 image, Pvt. Eugene Yoakum (left) and Mucho observe as Pvt. Robert Key coaches his partner through the obstacle course. Yoakum, seen in 1962 encouraging Mucho in a parking lot along Duke Street, trained Mucho to respond to radio commands. The dog wore a small citizens-band receiver on his harness and would respond only to Yoakum's voice. This allowed the team to be more flexible, with Mucho able to work without a lead.

The Canine Corps had special training and housing needs, so the department set up the facility seen below around 1970. Teams like Pvt. Ronald Ramsey and Prince, in this photograph from about 1972, spent hours each week exercising and training at the K-9 facility, which was equipped with kennels, an obstacle course, and a small house for classroom training. Kennels were very important because, although dogs were allowed to live with officers, they had to be securely boarded when the officers were out of town. The kennel later moved from this location, south of Duke Street near Wheeler Avenue, to South Payne Street. Plans call for the new police headquarters to be built on a location near the old kennel site.

Alexandria's Canine Corps gained respect from other law enforcement agencies, who sent their officers and dogs to Alexandria for training. Sgt. Cecil Kesler remained with the unit for more than a decade, and after King retired, Kesler (far right) partnered with Prince and continued teaching dozens of officers and dogs. In a photograph from about 1967 (below), Kesler (second from left) watches another class of K-9 handlers graduate as Inspector George Everly (third from left) presents the officers with their certificates. Of particular note are the uniform shoulder patches. The Canine Corps had its own patch throughout the 1960s, but members of today's K-9 unit simply wear the traditional department patch.

Officers were proud to protect Gerald R. Ford when he suddenly became president of the United States in August 1974. Ford and his family had lived at 514 Crown View Drive in Alexandria since 1955. Richard M. Nixon announced his resignation and Ford was sworn in the next day, but 11 days passed before the Ford family moved into the White House. Until then, Alexandria officers, many with special tactical training, assisted the Secret Service with security, restricted traffic, and escorted the new president into Washington. To the president's left are, from left to right, officers Randy Benarick, Roscoe Price, Ralph Carlton, and Robert "Pete" Moss, and to his right are, from left to right, officers Marcel Minutolo and James Butts, Lt. Walter Calhoun, and Sgt. Ronald Graves. In 2001, another generation of Alexandria officers volunteered to work at George W. Bush's first inauguration.

Once several officers had received extensive training in tactical methods, the department formally established its Special Operations Team in the mid-1970s. Known as SOT, the group was equipped with powerful firearms and protective gear and responded to hostage situations and other critical incidents. In a 1982 photograph, SOT members surround the entrance to a bank in Fairlington where two robbers had taken an employee hostage. The stand-off ended without injury when the victim was released and the suspects surrendered. Firearms training is a priority for SOT members, photographed below at the range around 1988. From left to right are (first row) Robert Dowling, James Ammons, Stephen O'Neal, Raleigh Harsley, Charles Hill, Douglas Powell, Peter Crawford, Edward Sarra, and Ronald Graves; (second row) David Hoffmaster, Anthony Syrowski, Monte Rosson, Jack Compton, and Andrew Chelchowski.

Going back to at least the 1800s, Alexandria has hosted large street parades for all occasions. Sometimes police marched as part of the processions, but often officers had to close roads, protect honored guests, and maintain crowd control. When Pres. Herbert Hoover attended the 1930 parade in honor of George Washington's birthday, an estimated 150,000 spectators turned out. In this image, a crowd assembled along North Fairfax Street directly in front of the police station. Officers can been seen standing in the middle of the street, maintaining order among the swelling crowd. In the late 1940s, about a dozen officers march west on King Street with shops visible in the 1100 block. This event too may well have been in celebration of Washington's birthday, a parade that is still held every February in his hometown. (Top image: Alexandria Library Special Collections.)

Lt. Henry Grimm leads junior officers and the police boys' band up North Washington Street in this parade in the early 1950s. The large white building in the background was a cotton factory in the mid-1800s and served as a prison during the Civil War. It later became a brewery and then an apartment building before the International Association of Chiefs of Police purchased it for their headquarters in 1992.

In 1964, the National Municipal League designated Alexandria as an All-America City, and Alexandria hosted its own celebration at the intersection of King and Washington Streets. Members of the police department's color guard assembled in front of the stage. The city was honored specifically for citizen involvement in community improvement. Alexandria won the award again in 1985.

Since its establishment in 1964, the police color guard has attended hundreds of official events such as parades, awards ceremonies, police funerals, dignitary visits, and city government functions. From left to right in this photograph from around 1967, color guard members Cpl. Joseph Robey, patrolman David Largen, Capt. Alfred Davis, and patrolmen Paul Harris and Clifford Church march down North Washington Street.

The color guard expanded into a full honor guard with a dozen officers by the early 1980s, when this photograph was taken. All were well trained in precision drills. From left to right are (first row) Gwen Robbins, Dana Lawhorne, James Ammons, Fred Akins, John Kochensparger, and Paul Story; (second row) Carl Petry, Michael Nicholson, Ralph Carlton, Chuck Charles, Herman Springs, and Mike Crabill.

Five

TRAFFIC SAFETY

In its first decades, the police department encountered accidents involving horses, trains, pedestrians, and the occasional bicycle. When motorized vehicles made their way onto Alexandria's roads, the police took steps to prevent crashes and arrest speeders. In 1911, police, without speedometers or even a car, began catching speeders. Officers with watches stood at the ends of two blocks while a car operating at the speed limit drove past and noted it took about 50 seconds. Officers then noted the speeds of other motorists and used signals to indicate which ones were speeding. When a motorcyclist covered the two blocks in less than 25 seconds, the officers arrested him for speeding. The man later paid a $10 fine. This system proved to be a success for catching speeders, though as cars became more common, accidents increased. A police officer investigates this 1931 crash on Washington Street at the railroad tracks.

Pvt. Ernest C. Suthard investigates a car crash with children watching him in this photograph taken around 1932. Suthard was a member of the motorcycle unit and responded to dozens of accidents in his early career. In one month alone in 1932, police issued 92 traffic citations and arrested four motorists for driving under the influence of liquor. That same month, crashes in Alexandria left one person dead and five more injured. The maximum speed limit in business districts was 15 miles per hour and 25 miles per hour in residential areas, and police increased enforcement to encourage motorists to drive more carefully. In an image from around 1941, Cpl. William Bayliss (left) and Pvt. Leslie Saunders (right) appeal to the public with a tally board outside of the police station that displays the number of traffic fatalities.

This accident in the 900 block of North Henry Street left one man dead and attracted spectators on both sides of the busy road. In early 1944, a speeding truck owned by a local fuel company collided with a larger one near the company's headquarters. A 43-year-old passenger in the fuel truck was thrown from the vehicle and killed. Police arrested the 22-year-old driver and charged him with involuntary manslaughter. Later that year, the fuel company, Slagle and Stark, and other local firms with fleets of vehicles participated in a traffic safety campaign sponsored by the Alexandria Safety Council. The fuel company's eight vehicles logged more than 80,000 miles and recorded three accidents in the year-long campaign. The winner was the Chesapeake and Potomac Telephone Company, whose 20 drivers traveled more than 112,000 miles in 15 vehicles without a single crash. The Alexandria Railway Express Agency and Colonial Laundry finished second and third respectively.

U.S. Route 1 runs through the eastern portion of Alexandria, and even before its official designation as a major national road, it was the frequent scene of car crashes. In the 1930s, two police officers, one from Alexandria and one from Arlington, were killed in separate accidents along the northern stretch then known as the Washington-Richmond Highway. A 1947 photograph shows where Pvt. William Gosney, a motor officer, marked the path of a vehicle with chalk as part of his investigation into a fatal accident. Another motor officer in 1960 had to direct traffic around an accident in the same area of Route 1, now known as Jefferson Davis Highway.

King and Washington Streets, two of Alexandria's oldest and busiest roads, intersect in the heart of downtown. The area has always been home to shops and other businesses and remains heavily traveled by pedestrians. In 1962, a driver lost control of his car and crashed into the Lerner store at the southeast corner. The car struck two teenage boys, one of whom later died of his injuries. The driver was arrested and charged with manslaughter but was later acquitted. Another 1962 accident at the same location involved a city fire truck, and officers directed traffic around the fire truck. No one was seriously injured in the nighttime crash.

In March 1969, a car fleeing from police crashed into a row house, causing part of the building to collapse. An unlicensed teenage girl ran a stop sign at North Fayette and Madison Streets and nearly struck a police car. The officer in that cruiser tried to get her to stop but she sped away. The officer pursued her, and the chase reportedly reached speeds more than 70 miles per hour. When the girl was unable to negotiate the turn from Henry Street to King Street, she lost control and crashed into 1024 King Street. The three-story house was unoccupied at the time but sustained extensive damage. Neither the driver nor her passenger, the owner of the car, suffered serious injuries. Police charged the driver with multiple traffic violations. In the 1990s, the department's pursuit policy was overhauled and now forbids officers from engaging in high-speed pursuits for traffic offenses.

Crashes were by no means limited to downtown Alexandria. In this photograph, Sgt. Ronald Graves, holding his flashlight and radio, interviews possible witnesses at the scene of a wreck in Del Ray while another officer assists. Multiple vehicles, including two police cruisers, were damaged in the accident at Commonwealth and East Mason Avenues, which captured the attention of dozens of residents one summer night in the late 1960s. In 1961, a single police cruiser crashed into a utility pole along Duke Street. This photograph was taken facing east on Duke Street around the 1800 block. Today this stretch of Duke Street, with four lanes and traffic signals at every block, serves as a gateway from the West End into Old Town with several medium-rise office buildings, upscale restaurants, and new hotels.

Traffic safety has always been a priority for police, and officers try to educate young people about stoplights, directional signals, and pedestrian safety. In the 1940s, Sgt. Henry Grimm, a motorcycle officer and traffic unit supervisor, set up a "mini" intersection for children in toy cars to practice safe driving. The course, laid out at the Jefferson School, featured an operating traffic light powered with automobile batteries. Grimm stood in the center of the "Tiny Town" intersection while another officer in the background assisted him. Children maneuvered through the intersection as others patiently waited for their green light. Some of the cars were marked by their sponsors, including the Alexandria Police Department, the Virginia State Police, and Herby's, a local car dealership. The Jefferson School opened in 1923 and was located on North West Street, facing Queen Street, near where Jefferson Village apartments now stand.

Officers actively involved children in traffic safety efforts, and the school safety patrol was one of the most popular activities. The program began around 1940, with separate programs for whites and blacks, as schools were segregated until the 1960s. The Alexandria School Boy Safety Patrol members participated in safety slogan contests and team sports. In the 1940s, safety patrol boys had their own baseball team, as their bus, the police paddy wagon, proudly announced. On May 6, 1956, thousands of police and schoolchildren celebrated the 20th anniversary of National School Safety Patrol Day with a parade in Washington, D.C. The boys from Alexandria wore replica police uniforms and white gloves as they marched with Lt. Henry Grimm down Constitution Avenue.

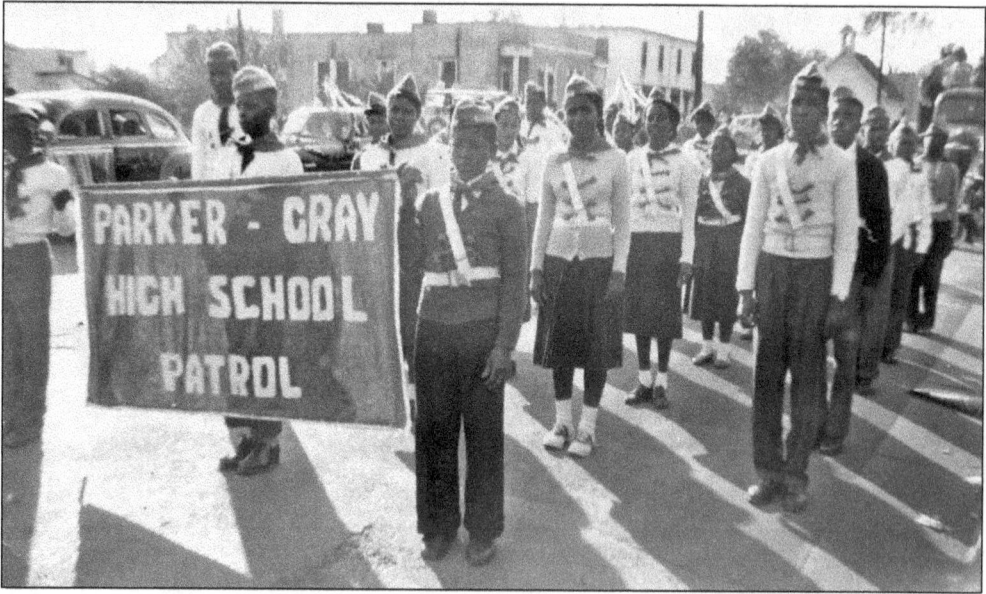

The safety patrol for Parker-Gray High School included boys and girls. Milton Stanton (center) holds the banner as students assemble in this 1940s image. In 1951, police hired 11 women, including three who were African American, as school crossing guards. This was the first time that either women or blacks publicly performed police duties in Alexandria. Hiring policewomen was a new concept in the Washington, D.C., suburbs at the time. Equipped with badges, white gloves, and whistles, the women wore police-style uniforms but with skirts and schoolboy patrol belts. Below at headquarters, Capt. Edgar Sims (center) joins the first crossing guards; from left to right are Janie C. Wright, Rosa Lee Stowers, Desiree Vass, ? Smythe, Blanche M. Kaiser, Elizabeth Cable, Alice B. Ross, Stella Pridgen, Edna V. Swiger, Dolores C. Reppel, and Marie W. Allen. (Top image: Alexandria Black History Museum.)

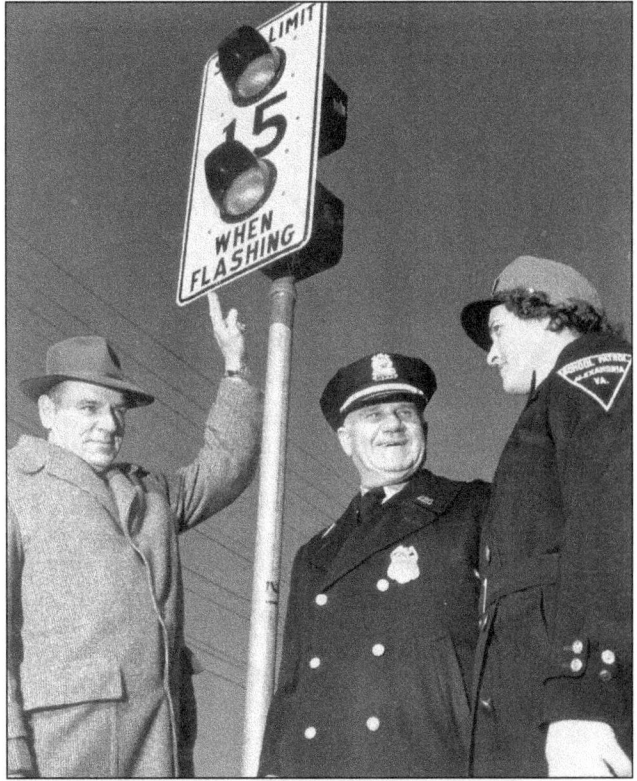

Police relied on both the school crossing guards and school patrol boys to keep children safe on their way to school. Flashing traffic signals and increased penalties for speeding in school zones were among the safety initiatives police welcomed. This publicity photograph from the early 1960s features Lt. Henry Grimm (center) and a school crossing guard. School patrol boys who completed their service were treated to a special outing at the end of the school year. In 1971, school crossing guard Trae Surina (far left) and Cpl. James Bazzle (back row, in uniform) took the safety patrol boys to the FBI headquarters in Washington, D.C., where former Alexandria officer John Cox (far right) gave them a tour of the shooting range.

As more cars filled the streets of Alexandria, parking became tighter and time limits were imposed. To enforce the restrictions, the city installed meters in 1940 and police officers were responsible for ticketing violators. In 1951, a few months after hiring women to work as crossing guards, the police department hired four women to monitor the meters. If ticketed, the violator faced a fine of $1. In a 1950s group photograph outside headquarters, the patrolwomen stand with other members of the traffic unit, including officers on motorcycles and one in a sidecar. In a 1962 image, Deputy Inspector James W. Baber and patrolwoman Katherine Grey watch patrolwoman Mary McCullough write a ticket.

To patrol congested downtown streets, parking enforcement staff walked or drove modified motorcycles. Full-sized cars were too expensive and blocked passing traffic, so three-wheeled vehicles offered the best option. Servi-Cars manufactured by Harley-Davidson provided the maneuverability of a motorcycle but were equipped with a storage trunk in the back. Their stability was a true safety benefit. A police officer has parked his Servi-Car and is issuing a ticket to a car in this 1972 photograph. By the 1980s, the parking fleet included a three-wheeled vehicle with an enclosed cab. This protected parking enforcement officers from the weather. In 1980, the enforcement staff of, from left to right, Avis Kirk, Mary McCullough, Renae Evans, Calvin Brent, Bonnie Lockhart, Frank Murphy, officer Charles Lloyd, and Cpl. Ronald Deitz stand with their vehicles in front of the George Washington Masonic National Memorial, commonly called the Masonic Temple.

Pvt. George Stinnett analyzes traffic concerns in this photograph from 1965. The police department first set up a system to record traffic accidents in 1927, and through analysis, police could better deploy resources and make safety recommendations. With the 1952 annexation of the West End came more traffic crashes and complaints. The data in Stinnett's chart indicates that two people were killed and 17 injured in a two-month period. The most common cause of accidents then were drivers under the influence of alcohol, following too closely, and failing to yield, and speeding and illegal turns were among the most common complaints. Stinnett's weekly staffing calendar showed the equal division of resources between downtown and the West End. A member of the Traffic Bureau for several years, Stinnett also served as the hack inspector and was responsible for checking the safety and lawful operation of taxi cabs. In the late 1960s, the designated cab inspection area was at Commonwealth and Cedar Avenues.

When Landmark Center opened in 1965, it was recognized as being the first shopping center in the Washington area to have three major department stores. Sears and the Hecht Company opened their doors to eager shoppers that summer, and Woodward and Lothrop followed in the fall. By the Christmas shopping season, traffic congestion and parking lots near capacity were signs of Landmark's retail success. Officers had to direct traffic along Duke Street to keep cars moving. Heavy traffic from the east and west can be seen in these 1965 images. In one photograph, the Lincolnia Motel can be seen on westbound Duke Street. The motel was the scene of a robbery and shooting in 1954. Robbers had targeted the Lincolnia and other motor lodges in a series of hold-ups but were captured in a police stakeout.

The use of radar proved to be one of the most effective methods in speed enforcement, and its results could be used as evidence in court. By the late 1960s, Alexandria had one radar unit and deployed it once or twice a week to areas where speeding was a common complaint. Even on a winter day in 1967, Pvt. Joseph Seiffert (in the police car) and two other officers caught a speeder on the snowy roads with radar. In another photograph, taken around 1971, motor officers are still using the large radar box, but they would soon switch to handheld radar guns. (Bottom image: Alexandria Library Special Collections.)

Six

SUPPORT AND
COMMUNITY SERVICES

Officers in the field have always depended upon support behind the scenes inside headquarters. Police administration supports communication systems, record keeping, community outreach, and personnel matters. One of the most critical functions is radio communication, which revolutionized police services after World War I. Alexandria's first radio car, seen in this photograph from the 1930s, received relays from the Metropolitan Police in Washington, D.C., by two-way radio. By 1933, Alexandria had three cars equipped with radios, and in 1939, the department was using three-way radios and its own dispatcher. This system allowed communication not only between headquarters and the cruisers but between the cruisers themselves. The use of radios increased police response to the public. In 1937, officers in a radio car rescued an Alexandria woman who tried to kill herself. The woman had struck herself on the head with a brick and collapsed on the railroad tracks on Wilkes Street. A witness telephoned police and a cruiser dispatched by radio reached the woman before the train arrived.

Improvement to Alexandria's radio system continued throughout the 1940s. A Teletype system, developed in the 1930s, enhanced communication among local police departments and across Virginia. When the department suffered staff shortages during World War II, it hired its first female employees. Rita L. Reynolds was the first, working as a clerk in the records room, and Marie Stephens was next, hired in 1944 to dispatch radio calls. By 1948, a new Motorola radio system was installed at the North Fairfax Street station, and these photographs were taken around that time. In the radio room are, from left to right, Cpl. Thomas McGowan, Pvt. Robert Peacher, and Pvt. Andrew Benarick. Using the keyboard of the Teletype machine, McGowan (at left) issued bulletins to neighboring jurisdictions and beyond.

The department's first switchboard was installed in the early 1950s, while headquarters was still on North Fairfax Street. In this image from 1951, Alice Guckert easily operates the switchboard, connecting emergency calls to the radio room and sending others to appropriate staff. She would continue to handle the main switchboard when the department moved to its North Pitt Street headquarters in 1959. Guckert retired in 1973. (Alexandria Library Special Collections.)

At the North Pitt Street station, officer Beverly Kennerly, like other officers, routinely worked shifts in the radio dispatch center. Kennerly stamped the time of a call on a card to record when the service request was dispatched. This photograph was taken in the late 1970s, before a regional 911 system was installed.

Clerks in the emergency communications center took calls from people needing police assistance. They would record the information on a card and then put the card on a moving track in the center of the console. The track carried the card into the radio room, where an officer would read it and dispatch a patrol unit to respond. Answering calls around 1978 are (clockwise from left) Diane Bowles, Karen Lowry, Carol Hensley, and Dorothy Weber. In the 1990s, after headquarters moved to Mill Road, emergency call takers used a system known as computer-aided dispatch. Jill Eastman, seen in this image from the mid-1990s, enters data as she speaks with callers.

Report writing evolved from a few notes on a shift log to half-page summaries to full forms called PD-7s. In this image from the early 1970s, Pvt. John Streeter uses an oversized template to point out the fields that officers have to complete for each offense they handle. Once a sergeant approved a report, it was sent to the records room. Staff in the records room were responsible for entering data about offenses and criminals. Both state and national crime databases store information about arrests and outstanding warrants. In the early 1970s, when the photograph below was taken, record clerks used a card punch system to document police and arrest data.

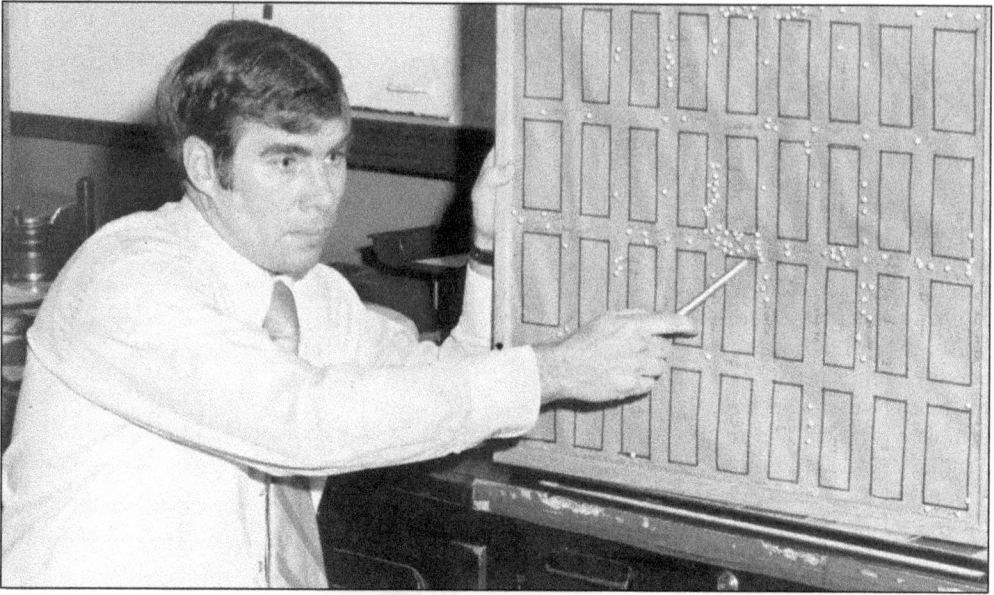

Administrative support staff have grown to rely heavily on computers, but in the late 1970s, a lot of work was still done by hand. Charles Moltz, a crime analyst, used a hand-drawn map and pushpins to indicate where a cluster of criminal activity occurred. In the 1990s, the department dedicated itself to improving its technology. In the late 1990s, Alexandria became one of the first departments to use completely mobile, wireless computers. Below Officer Timothy Kyburz demonstrates the tactical computer system that, through later modifications, allowed officers to write paperless reports, check state and national criminal databases, confirm vehicle information, and receive calls for service electronically.

Alexandria police tried to educate and involve the public about important safety issues. Officers met with civic organizations and encouraged awareness through public displays. These images from the 1950s, one with Lt. Henry Grimm (left) and Cpl. Ronald Mullen (right), show the variety of display materials. The showcases included antique and contemporary police weapons, restraint devices, and radio equipment. They also feature posters from slogan contests and charts with accident, crime, and arrest data. In one image, a map of Alexandria shows the city divided by census tracts. String from each tract led to a board with information about crime for each section of the city. Police still capture and analyze crime data according to census tracts.

Officers worked closely with Alexandria's schools and recreation centers, teaching children about traffic safety, the dangers of drugs and alcohol, and abduction prevention. In 1971, two officers visit with children outside Jefferson-Houston Elementary School. Cpl. James Bazzle (second from left) offers safety tips to Rodney Jones while officer Alfred Washington talks with Tammy Snead. Officer Donald Hayes, seen below playing chess with an Alexandria girl around 1988, worked with young people while in the crime prevention unit. Hayes later became an ordained pastor and serves as the police department's chaplain. Today specially trained school resource officers work full-time in Alexandria's public schools.

After Pres. John F. Kennedy designated the week of May 15 National Police Week in 1962, the police department began a community-awareness effort to educate the public about their agency. Police Week offered an opportunity for a public display, like this one from the early 1960s. For many years, the department had a special advertising supplement in the *Alexandria Gazette*, the local newspaper, during Police Week. In the 1970s, Lt. Andre Salvas reminded the public of the unique partnership between police and the public with a message decal on his cruiser. Andy Salvas, as he was known, retired as a captain in 1991.

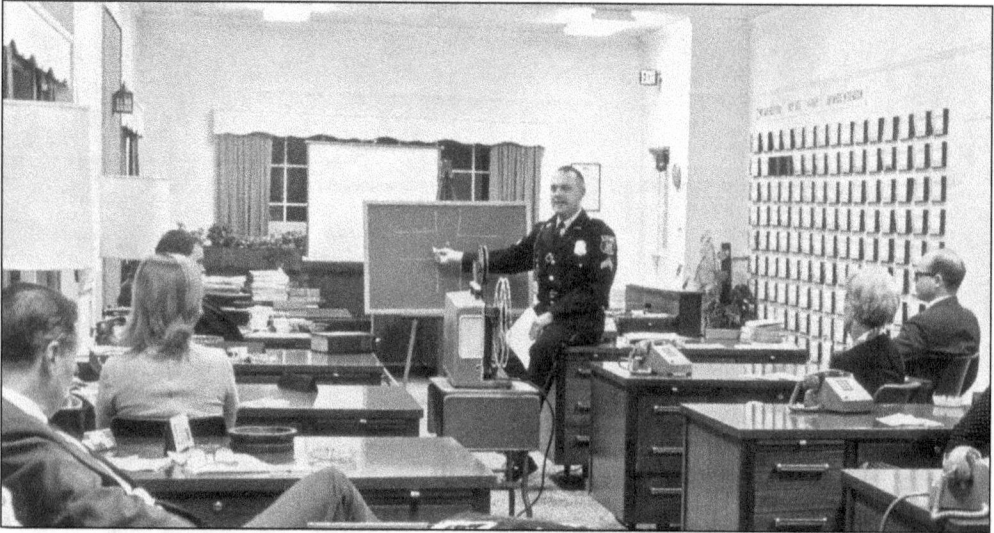

A strong relationship with the business community is a priority for the police department. Officers provide training about robbery awareness and other safety issues to local stores and restaurants. In the 1960s, Cpl. James Bazzle, the department's safety officer, met with real estate agents at their workplace. He showed a film and discussed good driving practices. Thirty years later, officer Mark Bergin and officer Dianne Gittins maintained a strong police presence along King Street, where Bergin worked closely with the businesses in Old Town. The Alexandria Chamber of Commerce has shown its appreciation for its police force by hosting annual valor awards honoring officers who demonstrate exceptional bravery.

Police administration is responsible for hiring and training the best police officer candidates. In 1936, the department held training sessions for those interested in joining the force. All candidates had to complete the school to be considered for appointment. Police commanders taught the classes on traffic control, use of weapons, crime classification, report writing, and crime prevention. Candidates who were hired to be officers had to pass a firearms certification. Pictured from left to right around 1947, recruit officers Jack Smith, George Grimm, and Bruce Proctor prepare to qualify with their weapons, in a shooting range in the basement of a plumbing shop near headquarters. Then Grimm, Proctor, and Smith fire as Cpl. Thomas McGowan uses binoculars to view their targets. All three were successful and began their police careers.

One of the earliest police cadets, Clyde Scott, receives his police officer uniform from Sgt. Robert Harlow in this photograph taken in 1959. The cadet program began in 1958 and continued for more than two decades. The training was the first of its kind in the metropolitan area and allowed young men interested in police careers to work inside the department. Cadets served in administrative assignments, learning technical skills and gaining exposure to traditional police work. Many cadets became police officers after turning 21. Cadet David Shepherd, seen in this late-1960s image, helped recruit others before becoming an officer himself.

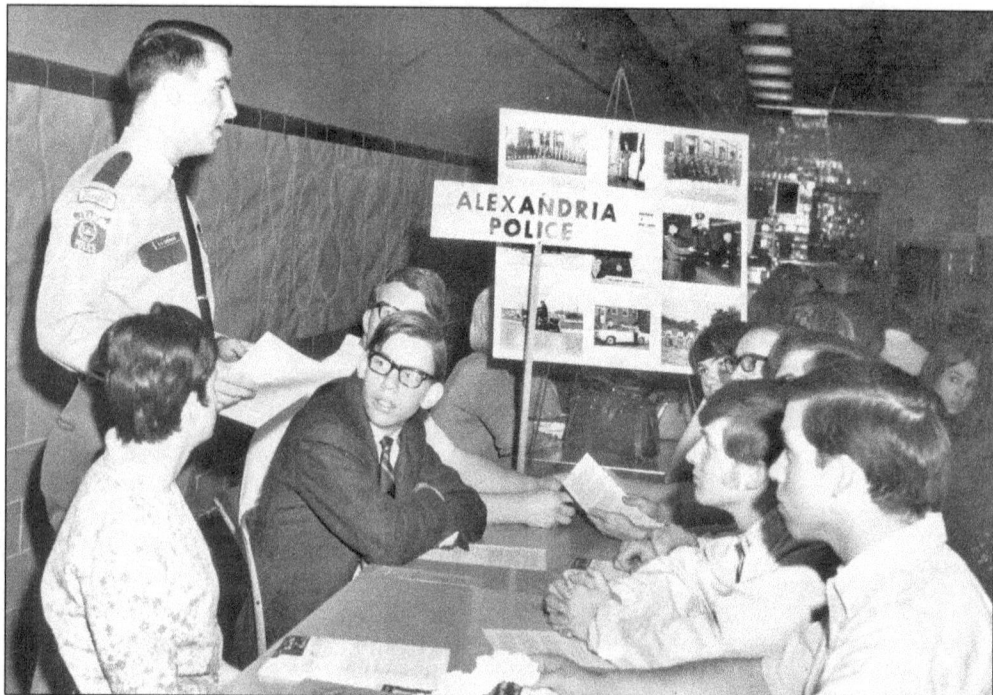

Department administrators oversee many duties, including recruiting, training, promotions, and planning. This hand-drawn advertisement from the 1960s featuring an officer with city hall in the background was designed to recruit police applicants. The starting pay for an Alexandria officer in 1965 was $5,425, and the department supplied the uniform and necessary equipment.

LAW ENFORCEMENT
A
PROFESSIONAL CAREER

POLICE DEPARTMENT CITY OF ALEXANDRIA, VA.

Officers received recognition for outstanding service. In 1971, in city council chambers, Chief John Holihan (far left) presents commendations to the following, from left to right: (first row) Pvt. Bruce Natterer, Sgt. Robert Key, Pvt. Elwood Schwartz, Sgt. Monroe K. Bryant, Pvt. Bruce Proctor, and Pvt. Stephen A. Martin; (second row) Pvt. John Morrison, Cpl. Joseph Seiffert, Pvt. John Stedman. Pvt. Perry Stephens, Pvt. Richard Moore, Pvt. Louis Pugh, and Pvt. Joseph Hilleary.

As law enforcement was professionalized in the later 20th century, a greater emphasis was placed on training, education, planning, and research. In the late 1960s, Cpl. Joseph Seiffert worked in the crime prevention and research office and assembled a library of law-enforcement publications and resources. In the mid-1980s, the department focused on national accreditation and in 1986 became one of the first police departments in the country to be accredited by the Commission on Accreditation for Law Enforcement Agencies. By undergoing this voluntary process, the Alexandria Police Department had to comply with more than 400 highly regarded standards. From left to right, Lt. Monroe Bryant, Capt. Joseph Seiffert, Chief Charles Strobel, Mayor James P. Moran, and city manager Vola Lawson applaud this achievement.

Seven

CHIEFS, FALLEN HEROES, AND TRAILBLAZERS

Capt. Charles T. Goods, the second chief of police, marches in a parade wearing a white cap (second from right) in this photograph taken near Prince and Washington Streets around 1916. Goods joined the department in 1896, became its chief in 1906, and retired in 1923. He later served as a detective with the Richmond, Frederick, and Potomac Railroad until he lost his leg in a railroad accident in 1946. In the same photograph is policeman Walker W. Campbell, holding a nightstick (third from left). Campbell joined the department in 1910, and in 1919, he was shot by a man he was trying to arrest about a block away from where this photograph was taken. The man had thrown an empty whiskey flask to the ground, and when Campbell began to take him to jail, the man pulled out a pistol and shot the officer. Campbell died two days later. (Alexandria Library Special Collections.)

When the Alexandria Police Department was officially organized in 1870, James F. Webster became its first chief, with the rank of captain, and earned $600 annually. Webster oversaw police operations, organized raids of gambling establishments, arrested drunks and murderers, and investigated thefts, shootings, and even grave robberies. He served as chief until 1906, when his health began to fail, but he remained as a desk sergeant until he died in 1910.

In 1887, policeman Julian Arnold, pictured in this drawing, was shot and killed by burglars. Arnold, a veteran of the Civil War, is the first Alexandria officer known to die in the line of duty. In 1893, policeman George W. Crump was shot in the leg by a fellow officer inside the police station. The accidental shooting proved to be tragic, as Crump died of his injury two months later.

Capt. Haywood J. Durrer was named chief in 1923, only months after he left Alexandria to be a Fairfax patrolman. One of Alexandria's first motorcycle officers, Durrer was seriously injured in a crash in 1919 but recovered and returned to duty around the time he was photographed holding his weapon with two unidentified men. He made dozens of traffic- and liquor-related arrests before briefly serving in Fairfax. As the Alexandria chief (below), Durrer vigorously enforced Prohibition and gambling laws. In 1925, Durrer left Alexandria again and rejoined Fairfax, rising to the rank of captain. He was again injured on duty when a hit-and-run driver struck him in 1936. He recovered and served three more years before his death in 1939. His son, William L. Durrer, later served for 17 years as the Fairfax County police chief.

Capt. William W. Campbell (center) was the son of fallen officer Walker Campbell, and he was named chief in 1925. He first joined the force in 1916 but left in 1924 and was working as a railroad detective when he was tapped to be chief. Campbell served as chief until 1931. In this photograph, taken around 1928, Campbell stands next to Sgt. Charles R. McClary (right), who was killed in the line of duty the next year. On the night of June 20, 1929, McClary and Sgt. Edgar Sims were investigating a liquor complaint on North Patrick Street when an armed man emerged from an alley. The man pulled a gun and fired at McClary, killing him. The murderer fled and eluded police for nearly four years. He was captured in Ohio after a woman there recognized his photograph from a detective magazine and alerted police. He later pleaded guilty to killing Charles McClary.

On September 4, 1930, Pvt. Whitfield W. Lipscombe was at a fire station in Del Ray when an alarm sounded. When firefighters responded for a brush fire near Four Mile Run, Lipscombe jumped on the back of the fire truck. Along Washington-Richmond Highway, the fire truck swerved to avoid a car and the truck overturned, crashing into a ditch. Lipscombe was thrown from the truck and killed.

Just three days after Private Lipscombe died, Pvt. August Perault Pierce, known as Perry to his fellow officers, found a robber near Four Mile Run. Pierce confronted the suspect, who then drew a gun. The two opened fire, exchanging at least 10 shots. Pierce suffered a gunshot wound to the chest and died at the scene, and the robber died a day later.

In the spring of 1928, the police baseball team was ready for a busy season. From left to right are (first row) Edgar Sims, Clarence McClary, James Bayliss, Jack McMenamin, Art Ludlow, and Charles Summa; (second row) Edgar Mayhugh, Charles McClary, Elton Hummer, Lester McMenamin, George Everly, William Brown, Slim Giles, Ernest Suthard, and Lawrence Padgett. Three members of this team later died in the line of duty. Sgt. Charles McClary died in 1929, and his brother, Cpl. Clarence J. McClary, was shot by a moonshiner in 1935 in Loudoun County after he and other Alexandria officers joined a posse there. Sgt. Elton B. Hummer was shot and killed by an unknown assailant on South Alfred Street on August 18, 1928, just a few months after this photograph was taken. Despite an exhaustive manhunt, the killer was never caught, and Hummer's murder remains unsolved.

Capt. John S. Arnold served as chief from 1931 to 1947 but took a leave of absence during World War II. He had this photograph of himself taken as part of his initiative to establish Alexandria's first "rogue's gallery" around 1935. Shortly after Alexandria's mug shot system was established, it paid off when a man caught in Alexandria was found to be an escaped inmate. (Alexandria Library Special Collections.)

Maj. Edgar J. Sims joined the department in 1925 and worked his way up the ranks before officially becoming chief in 1947. He was one of the first detectives and also served as acting chief during World War II. In 1945, he was elected president of the Virginia Association of Chiefs of Police. Sims retired as chief in 1952.

Pvt. Robert B. Harris had worked as a radio technician before joining the police department on August 23, 1948. His expertise with radios was expected to be an asset to the force, but he never got the chance. On September 11, 1948, Harris and another officer were checking businesses along North Washington Street when Harris interrupted a burglar behind the Howard Johnson's restaurant. The burglar fatally shot Harris and then ran away. The killer was captured several months later. Harris had served less than three weeks when he died. Officers protected the alley where the crime occurred and a chalk circle marks the area when the young officer was slain.

Maj. Russell A. Hawes became chief in 1952 after heading the detective bureau for more than a decade. Hawes, a former boxer and semi-professional football player, joined the department in 1931 and soon began working on major cases. In 1937, Hawes graduated from the FBI National Academy, the first Washington, D.C., area officer to do so. As chief, Hawes saw the department through a period of significant growth that included the West End annexation in 1952, the move to a new headquarters in 1959, the establishment of the Northern Virginia Police Academy in 1965, and the planning of the pistol range, which opened in 1970. Hawes retired in early 1970 after reaching the mandatory retirement age of 65. This image of Hawes testing a new radio was taken in 1966 at an International Association of Chiefs of Police conference.

Pvt. Bobby G. Padgett, photographed with his daughter, joined the department in 1957. On February 4, 1959, he responded to South West Street for an assault. He encountered the suspect, and as he and another officer tried to handcuff the man, a struggle ensued. The suspect broke free, grabbed Padgett's pistol, and shot him twice, killing him. The man was captured and later received the death penalty.

Deputy Inspector James W. Baber (first row, second from right), known as "Bootie" to his friends, suffered a fatal heart attack in 1962 after subduing a suspect involved in a bar fight near Queen and Fayette Streets. Baber became an officer in 1935 and was extremely active in sports organizations, especially with the police youth camp. He took over traffic enforcement operations in 1960, shortly after he was photographed with fellow commanders.

On October 1, 1965, Pvt. Albert Beverly, a 24-year-old from Virginia's Northern Neck, was sworn in as an Alexandria police officer. In doing so, Beverly became the first African American to serve as a police officer in Alexandria or in any of the major departments in the Washington, D.C., suburbs. Nearly two years later, he was still the only minority officer in the suburbs. Known as Al, Beverly worked in patrol before being named to the police community relations team in 1969. The team was formed to improve the police department's relationship with the public and, in particular, with the African American community. Beverly served in the youth bureau, investigating cases involving juveniles, and later returned to patrol before retiring in 1985.

Pvt. Eugene Yoakum, a K-9 handler, was slain on September 27, 1964, on Seay Street. Yoakum, who joined the department in 1954, observed a man holding a knife but with the other hand behind his back. When Yoakum tried to talk to him, the suspect brought his hidden hand forward and he was holding a gun. He opened fire, killing Yoakum. Other officers returned fire and killed the suspect.

In 1970, after serving 28 years with the Syracuse Police Department in New York, John B. Holihan became Alexandria's police chief, following Maj. Russell Hawes. Under Holihan's command, the department commissioned a study from the International Association of Chiefs of Police on ways to improve the force. He also added a tactical team, which later grew into the Special Operations Team. Holihan retired in 1977.

Det. Conrad L. Birney was killed in a bank robbery on December 27, 1972. Birney, who had first joined the department in the late 1950s, worked in youth investigations and regularly dressed in plain clothes. When the robbery call went out on Kenmore Avenue, Birney was nearby and quickly responded. As he entered the bank carrying his handheld radio, the suspects were leaving, and they encountered each other in the doorway. He and the robbers saw each other at the same time and the robbers recognized the radio as a police radio. Before Birney could seek cover or even draw his weapon, one of the robbers fired at him. The bullet hit Birney in the chest and as he fell, he drew his weapon. But the suspects fled, and he was unable to return fire and died a short time later. All three suspects were later captured, tried, and convicted.

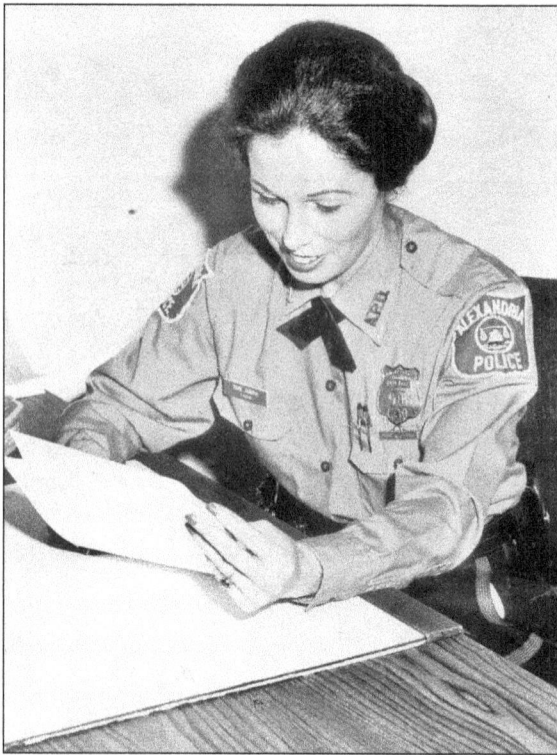

Trae Surina worked as a crossing guard for four years but wanted to be a police officer. Other women handled youth investigations but were not patrol officers. In 1972, Surina broke that barrier, becoming the first woman to be a full-fledged officer. An expert marksman who graduated first in her academy class, Surina enjoyed a successful career. Trae Heath, as she was then known, retired as a lieutenant in 1999.

In 1974, Gwendolyn Robbins became the first African American woman to be an Alexandria police officer. Several minority women in the community affectionately called Robbins "Christie Love" after the title character on a television show about a black undercover policewoman. Robbins, like Heath, earned respect as well as several promotions. She retired in 1996, a few years after this photograph was taken, as a lieutenant.

Charles T. Strobel was named chief in August 1977 after Chief Holihan announced his retirement. Strobel joined the force in 1958 and rose steadily through the ranks. In 1983, the city manager appointed Strobel as the public safety director, a new position overseeing police, firefighting, and code enforcement. The consolidation of public safety operations ended in 1986, and Strobel remained police chief until his retirement in December 1987.

Gary J. Leonard was named chief in the spring of 1988. Leonard came to Alexandria after working for several police departments in the western part of the country. Leonard tried to target drug-related crime and budget challenges, but after two years, he resigned to become chief of a Utah police department.

On March 22, 1989, an escapee from a Washington, D.C., halfway house took several people hostage at 316 Hopkins Court to collect a drug debt. Dozens of officers responded, and as hostage negotiators attempted to get the armed man's cooperation, the Special Operations Team moved into position. Officers assumed strategic positions throughout the housing project, and when the suspect emerged, he was holding a sawed-off shotgun to the head of a teenager. A sharpshooter fired and struck the gunman but he was able to fire two shots before police killed him. Those shots struck two Special Operations Team members, Cpl. Charles W. Hill and officer Andrew M. Chelchowski. Hill was pronounced dead on arrival at the hospital. At least 2,000 people, including police from throughout Virginia and as far away as New York, attended Hill's funeral.

Corporal Hill had served as a New York City police officer before coming to Alexandria in 1976. Charlie, as he was called by his fellow officers, worked in patrol and later as an identification technician. He joined the Special Operations Team, and in 1980, he became the firearms instructor at the police range. He was fatally shot in 1989 in the same incident that critically injured officer Chelchowski. Chelchowski became an Alexandria officer in 1977 and in 1983 joined the K-9 unit, where he worked with his partner, Vader; they are photographed together below receiving an award. Chelchowski suffered gunshot wounds to his legs but was later able to return to full duty and to his job as a K-9 handler. He died in 1993.

Charles E. Samarra, a 23-year veteran of the Metropolitan Police Department in Washington, D.C., was sworn in as chief in 1990 by Edward Semonian, the clerk of court. Under Samarra's leadership, the Alexandria Police Department implemented community-based policing initiatives, increased the diversity of its staff, and established citizen police academies to educate the public about police functions. He also oversaw the modernization of the department's technology, with mobile computers for every officer and an overhaul of the radio and 911 center. During this same time, Alexandria experienced a significant decrease in serious crime. Samarra, Alexandria's 11th police chief, announced his retirement in the summer of 2006.

Eight

OFF-DUTY

Even when Alexandria police officers were not officially on duty, their activities often centered on the Alexandria community. In the late 1880s, police hosted annual balls at Lannon's Opera House. A newspaper account describes the 1885 police ball as the "largest and most enjoyable affair of the kind ever before given" in Alexandria. Ticket sales from police balls raised money to purchase new uniforms and hats, which officers had to pay for themselves. Lannon's Opera House opened in 1884 and was located on the southwest corner of King and Pitt Streets. A saloon operated on the first floor of the building, and the second story, with a high ceiling and long windows, was home to the opera house and was used as an event hall. Sometime in the 20th century, a bowling alley opened on the spacious second floor. The brick building was demolished in 1969.

115

Officers often took part in organized sports, and baseball was the most popular for decades. From the early 1920s until the start of World War II, the department fielded highly competitive teams. Alexandria police played against teams from the *Alexandria Gazette*, *Washington Post*, Potomac Yard railyard, Metropolitan Police Department, and local fire stations. Sometimes the games were used as special fund-raisers to help the family of an injured or fallen policeman or firefighter. The city manager and chief joined the players and ballboy for the 1937 team portrait at Baggett Stadium. Pictured from left to right are (first row) Earl Watkins, Henry Grimm, Claude Nixon, Edgar Sims Jr., Robert A. Brenner, Francis Johnson, and Frank Stover; (second row) city manager Emmett C. Dunn, Edgar Sims, Willie Schwartz, Buddy Zimmerman, Lawrence Padgett, Eugene Zimmerman, Clarence Wilkie, and John Arnold, chief of police.

From the 1960s to present, officers have remained active in sports, whether for recreation, a good cause, or both. In 1968, the police softball team won the city championship, and in the early 1970s, the department fielded a football team. Above from left to right are (first row) Alvin Dodd, Joseph Hilleary, Ralph Carlton, Walter Calhoun, Ronald Giovannucci, and P. Powers; (second row) Junior Bowling, John Streeter, Larry Black, Randy Benarick, William Wieland, Curtis Eaby, and Wayne Robey. In the 1990s, officers got involved with the Torch Run, an annual fund-raiser for the Special Olympics. Twenty-five officers took part in the charity run in 2000.

Many officers served in the military, and John S. Arnold (right), police chief and World War I veteran, was on National Guard duty at the Alexandria armory in the 1930s. Capt. Walter Cameron Roberts (left) and 1st Lt. William Milton Glasgow (center) commanded Company I, 1st Infantry, of the Virginia National Guard, known locally as the Alexandria Light Infantry. Glasgow, a railroad employee, was a volunteer fireman in Alexandria and later became a magistrate. This photograph was taken inside the armory on South Royal Street. Built in 1876, the armory not only housed military equipment but also was later used as a lounge for service members during World War II and as a community recreation center during peacetime. In 1953, a large fire started in the armory while guard units were serving in Korea. The fire destroyed the armory, though the ammunition was protected in a steel and concrete vault. (Alexandria Library Special Collections.)

In the late 1920s, police officers began a fund and organization to support each other and community efforts. This group became the Alexandria Police Association (APA) and hosted activities and events for officers, their families, and the community. The APA crab pick soon became a favorite event. From left to right in 1950, Lt. Russell Hawes, Sgt. James W. Baber, Pvt. Thomas McGowan, local teacher Frank Marino, Pvt. Charles L. Baber, councilman James M. Duncan, Mayor Franklin Backus, and Maj. Edgar Sims feasted at the Cameron Club. A month after becoming president, Gerald Ford attended the police crab pick. Ford and members of the American and Soviet space programs eventually got the hang of crab picking. In the image at right, Det. Joseph Serafin demonstrated his mallet technique to the new president while astronaut Thomas Stafford (far left) and cosmonaut Vladimir Shatalov (right of Ford) looked on.

Several officers have shared their musical talents with appreciative audiences. In the 1940s and 1950s, the police department had a band that performed in parades and at community events. In this early-1950s photograph, a band supporter (far right) directs two members, Cpl. Ronald Mullen on the xylophone and Lt. Henry Grimm with the tuba. At least two police officers were members of the Washington Redskins marching band, and several others played with local bands at parties. Sgt. Edgar Cassady played guitar, as did Sgt. Cecil Kesler, seen playing lead guitar with a country band in a photograph from the early 1970s.

In 1946, the Alexandria Police Association supported a plan by Sgt. Henry Grimm to open a camp for the boys of Alexandria. It set aside $2,000, authorized a board of directors, and approved of plans to borrow money to purchase land. The board selected a site along the water in Kilmarnock in Virginia's Northern Neck. They raised additional money through a public campaign to build cabins and bath facilities for the campers. In the summer of 1946, some 125 city boys enjoyed vacations in the country at the police camp. Camp officials were eager to show supporters the dock and boats. In 1947, the camp was officially organized as the Alexandria Police Boys' Camp and named Camp Charles Herbert Grimm in honor of Sergeant Grimm's son, who had been killed in Iwo Jima during World War II.

Boys ages 8 to 15 spent two weeks at the camp each summer and took part in a variety of outdoor activities. The camp's location along the Chesapeake Bay offered campers the opportunity to boat, swim, fish, and crab. Campers hiked and participated in archery, boxing, football, soccer, baseball, volleyball, and even Ping-Pong. At night, the boys and counselors sat around a campfire and told stories or watched a movie in the recreation hall. In the early 1950s, more than 700 boys went to the camp each summer. No family was permitted to pay while their son was at camp; however, many families later made generous donations to the camp fund. In this way, families of limited financial means were able to see their sons experience the same outdoor fun as other boys.

Officers found tremendous support in Alexandria for the camp. Civic organizations and local businesses donated money, sporting equipment, and supplies. The AB&W Transit Company donated buses to transport boys from Alexandria to the camp, and for many years, Herby's Ford donated a new station wagon, like this one in 1957. Individuals and civic groups funded new cabins, and other buildings, like a mess hall, boathouse, and recreation facility, were erected within a few years of the camp's opening. Plaques on buildings honored sponsors like the Alexandria Fire Department and Kiwanis Club, who funded this cabin. Each summer, the camp hosted Civic Club Day, and citizens and community leaders traveled to the camp to see the work being done there. Visitors went on a tour of the grounds and a boat ride before enjoying a large dinner.

Many of the boys who attended the camp stayed active with related organizations throughout the year. In 1952, the Alexandria Police Association organized the Alexandria Police Boys' Band to give musically talented boys the chance to study music and perform in public settings. When it was first established, the band had 63 members. This photograph was taken in 1953 at one of the band's earliest performances.

The camp's board of directors in 1954 were, from left to right, Sgt. Robert A. Brenner, Capt. James W. Baber, Lt. Henry F. Grimm, Cpl. Thomas J. McGowan, Sgt. William Bayliss, and Pvt. Marshall S. Snyder. Board members were responsible for hosting Civic Club Day tours, publicity and fund-raising campaigns, and fiscal matters.

In the 1950s, the camp benefited from ticket sales from antique shows. Today some local restaurants donate a portion of their receipts during special events. For many years, the camp has also raised money by selling Christmas trees at Union Station. Santa Claus and others join Lt. Joseph Hilleary at the annual Christmas tree sale in this image from the early 1990s.

In the fall of 2003, Hurricane Isabel caused extensive damage to the dock and several buildings, but officers and volunteers worked hard to make repairs. Though counselors work throughout the summer, many officers spend their days off and vacation time at the camp. Now in its 60th year, Camp Grimm continues to offer healthy outdoor activities and a taste of country living to Alexandria's children.

The Alexandria Police Association has remained committed to supporting the families of their officers and those in the community. In the 1980s and 1990s, the association prepared and served traditional Thanksgiving meals for Alexandria's seniors, and in 1971, the association hosted a special day for children at Landmark Mall. Ready to serve cold beverages are, from left to right, Lt. James Hill, Pvt. John Streeter, and Cpl. Joseph Seiffert. In an image from the late 1950s, association president Norman Grimm (center) helps Santa Claus hand out gifts to the children of officers at a holiday party at the Elks Club on Prince Street. Santa still visits children each December at the police association hall.

The Alexandria Police Association honors its retirees with dinner banquets. In 1965, Mayor Frank Mann (left), Maj. Russell Hawes (center), and Albert Hair (right), the city manager, congratulate retiring officers Richard Woody (seated left) and Henry Grimm (seated right). That year, officers' wives prepared the dinner, which was held at the Second Presbyterian Church. Even after their official police careers end, many retirees remain active. In 1968, retired lieutenant Warren Zimmerman organized a group of retirees to meet for lunch dates. Though Zimmerman died that year, the group continued to meet and the next year invited retired firefighters to join them. In 1969, they established the Alexandria Retired Police and Fire Association, which continues to host luncheons, holiday parties, and charitable events. In 1978, nearly two dozen retired police employees attended a reception in their honor when this photograph was taken at headquarters.

DISCOVER THOUSANDS OF LOCAL HISTORY BOOKS FEATURING MILLIONS OF VINTAGE IMAGES

Arcadia Publishing, the leading local history publisher in the United States, is committed to making history accessible and meaningful through publishing books that celebrate and preserve the heritage of America's people and places.

Find more books like this at
www.arcadiapublishing.com

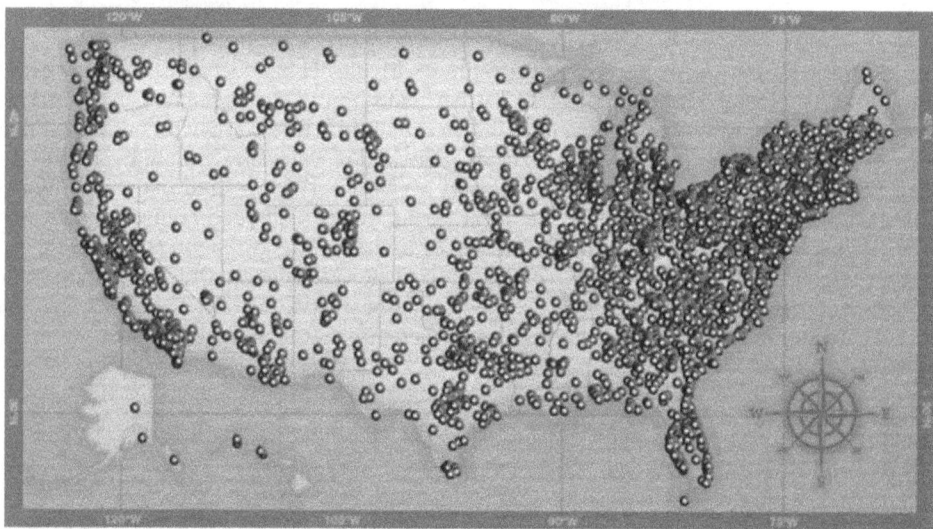

Search for your hometown history, your old stomping grounds, and even your favorite sports team.

Consistent with our mission to preserve history on a local level, this book was printed in South Carolina on American-made paper and manufactured entirely in the United States. Products carrying the accredited Forest Stewardship Council (FSC) label are printed on 100 percent FSC-certified paper.

MADE IN THE USA